308.02
Eve

HOW TO WRITE A TERM PAPER

HOW TO WRITE A TERM PAPER

REVISED EDITION

BY NANCY EVERHART

A SPEAK OUT, WRITE ON! BOOK
Franklin Watts
New York   Chicago   London   Toronto   Sydney

To Madge Hutcherson and the Florida State University
School of Library and Information Studies

Photographs copyright ©: Comstock Inc./Bonnie Kamin: p. 8; Monkmeyer
Press Photo: pp. 17 (Rhoda Sydney), 59, 81, 118 (all Hugh Rogers), 70
(Michael Kagan), 72 (Rick Kopstein); Photo Researchers Inc.: pp. 22
(F. B. Grunzweig), 32 (Laima Druskis), 54 (Will McIntyre); Ben Klaffke:
pp. 28, 87; Jay Mallin: pp. 37, 39, 42, 45, 64; Grolier Multimedia:
p. 49.

Library of Congress Cataloging-in-Publication Data

Everhart, Nancy.
    How to write a term paper / by Nancy Everhart.—Rev. ed.
        p.   cm.—(A Speak out, write on! book)
    Rev. ed. of: So you have to write a term paper! 1987.
    Includes bibliographical references and index.
    Summary: Describes the steps in writing a term paper, including
choosing a topic, doing research, writing an outline, taking notes,
doing a rough draft, and editing the final paper.
    ISBN 0-531-11200-4 (lib. bdg.)
    1. Report writing.   2. Research.   [1. Report writing.
2. Research.]   I. Everhart, Nancy. So you have to write a term
paper! II. Title. III. Series.
LB1047.3.E94   1994   94-29385 CIP AC

CONTENTS

Chapter One
To the Reader
9

Chapter Two
What Is a Term Paper? Why Write One?
12

Chapter Three
Topics for Term Papers
15

Chapter Four
A Plan of Attack: An Outline and Identification
of Key Terms
30

Chapter Five
The Library's Reference Sources
36

Chapter Six
Primary Sources
68

Chapter Seven
The Working Bibliography
74

Chapter Eight
The Outline
79

Chapter Nine
Taking Notes
86

Chapter Ten
A Little Lecture on Writing
95

Chapter Eleven
Organizing Your Information and Writing
the Rough Draft
102

Chapter Twelve
How to Cite References
113

Chapter Thirteen
Revising the Rough Draft; Writing the Final Draft
122

Checklist for Completion
133

For Further Reading
135

Index
137

HOW TO WRITE A TERM PAPER

Inevitably—and probably more than once through your school career—a teacher will assign a term paper.

ONE

𝒯O THE READER

The inevitable has happened: you have been assigned a term paper. If you are like many students, your palms may start to sweat, your heart may race, your throat may constrict. You are, plain and simple, scared. Even if you aren't scared, admit it: you feel just a little nervous. You also may feel annoyed about all that time you will have to spend on the assignment.

When the assignment was given, probably your whole class groaned. Take heart, then: you're not alone in your fears, or minor anxiety, or annoyance. In fact, since all students have to write term papers at one time or another, whether they are in elementary school or college, you've got a lot of company. They number in the millions.

This book tells you what a term paper is and shows you how to write a good one. Information on using a computer in your task is included, because there's a good chance you have access to one.

Using a computer will make your job easier, but you can still write a perfectly decent paper without one. Lots of term papers were written before the introduction

Where Computers Can Help

TOPIC SELECTION

Americana Topic Finder and Research Planner

CD-ROM Indexes

On-line Catalog

INFORMATION GATHERING

CD-ROM Indexes

Full-text Databases

On-line Catalogs

On-line Databases

Notebook Computer

WRITING

Database, Word Processing or Integrated Software Programs

Bibliography Program

Term Paper Program

Spelling Checker

Grammar Checker

Scanner to integrate photographs or illustrations

Graphing program

of computers, and lots more are bound to be. At the same time, using a computer won't guarantee you an A. Reading *How to Write a Term Paper* will provide you with the knowledge you need to overcome the fears—or minor anxiety—you might have. It will also help you to turn a required assignment into one you meet head-on in anticipation of pleasure, not boredom or drudgery.

SUPER STRATEGIES

1. Start the assignment early rather than waiting until the week before the paper is due. Divide your time into three blocks: (a) choosing the topic, (b) doing research, and (c) writing. The first block is the shortest; the last two will probably be equally long.
2. Ask your teacher questions, either in class or in private, about anything you aren't sure of, from the color of the paper you have to use to the fine points of the topic.

TWO

WHAT IS A TERM PAPER? WHY WRITE ONE?

A term paper is usually assigned to encourage you to learn more about a subject and to test various skills you may have learned in a class. Your teacher may want to see what you have learned or can learn about a subject, or to see if you can think critically, do research, or write effectively—or all of these.

Term papers are often assigned at the beginning of a class. Sometimes they count for a major part of your grade. If you go to college, you will find out that in some classes the term paper may be the only graded assignment you receive. In fact, your final grade may be based entirely on your paper and on the final exam.

Doing a good job on your term paper will not only help you get a good grade in your classes now but will also help you do well in college. Of course, there is more to life than grades. That's why it's important to work in such a way that you are actually interested in what you are doing. If you have a choice of topics, this means choosing an interesting topic—interesting to you.

ORIGINALITY

Few teachers expect papers of earthshaking originality, but they do want something with some evidence of original thinking. They want you to use your brain. Many students simply rehash material already adequately covered in encyclopedia articles.

The nature of your term paper will, of course, be influenced by any special instructions from your teacher. There are three main types of term papers: The first kind consists of your ideas about something or somebody—for example, your criticism of a new novel by Stephen King, or your interpretation of a short story by Ernest Hemingway. The second kind is a new interpretation of a body of knowledge—for example, your theory that the dinosaurs were not wiped out by a meteorite but instead by a volcanic eruption. The third kind consists of a bulk of information assembled in a new way—for example, a comparison of the plots in silent films with those in talkies. Each of these types of papers should reflect some original thinking.

It is likely that you have presented an opinion or interpretation before, and that you have organized facts. What distinguishes a term paper from an essay is the body of facts you provide to support your views; you aren't just going to spout your opinions. Similarly, you won't just list facts; you are going to interpret similarities and differences, and put pieces of information together in a meaningful way.

A term paper has to involve research. Your topic has to lend itself to detective work to uncover the information you need to criticize, interpret, assemble, and compare. Although most research for term papers is done in libraries, research also can be done through interviews, experimentation, and surveys. Sometimes, in fact, the best way to learn about a new field (like cryptozoology) is to talk to an expert. Still, most of your research will involve information gathered from printed matter and, in some cases, from computers, video-discs, filmstrips, videotapes, and other sources.

Your term paper is probably not going to win you a Pulitzer Prize or a Nobel Prize, although it might be the first step in a career leading to one. But it will help you learn how to think and how to work with information, extremely important talents in an age in which we are deluged with information about everything from AIDS to Zambia.

Now that you have a slightly better idea of the nature of a term paper, you may feel a little less anxious about your assignment and a little more excited about learning how to choose and work with term-paper topics.

SUPER STRATEGY

See if your teacher or library media center has a file of past term papers, so you will have an idea of what one looks like. Find those that were judged to be excellent and make a list of what seems to have made them good. Keep this list handy when working on your own paper.

THREE

ṪOPICS FOR TERM PAPERS

Topics for term papers are either assigned or left to you to choose—or some combination of the two. If you have been assigned a very specific topic and have no voice whatsoever in the matter, you might want to move on to the next chapter, although there is useful information here.

CHOOSE A TOPIC THAT INTERESTS YOU

You will do a better job on your paper—and have more fun—if you choose a topic that interests you, that really interests you.

Many assigned topics are very general. Your history teacher may want you to do research on the 1960s. You will have to decide exactly what to write about. Or your science class may be covering a unit on whales. You have to write on some aspect of whales, but the specific choice of what topic to write about is yours.

These assignments give you less leeway than the assignment to just "write a history term paper." But if you use your imagination and don't get bogged down in thinking, "Oh, the Vietnam War is boring" or "I don't know what to say about whales," you will be ahead of many of your classmates.

A good way to approach either type of assignment—restricted or unlimited—is to try to relate the topic to a hobby or interest, or to approach the topic through your own interests. If you are interested in women's issues, you could turn a report on Japan into a study of the changing role of women in Japanese society. A drawing enthusiast could write about famous black artists for a paper on African Americans. A more challenging topic might be an investigation of the role of black artists in the art world, or an attempt to answer the question, "Is there such a thing as a 'black style' in America?"

Here are other examples of ways to focus your paper on a particular interest of your own:

- A biology report could investigate toxic wastes in your community.
- A history paper could describe life in your community before and after cable television.
- A chemistry report could focus on the cosmetics industry.
- An English paper could probe into a writer's background to find out if a tragic love affair affected his or her poetry.

When selecting your topic, you'll probably want to visit the library, to see if the subject really interests you, to check whether there is material available, and to make sure the topic is suitable for a term paper.

Make sure that, if you choose something based on one of your pet interests, the subject is worth writing about and can be researched. "In-line Skating" could be frivolous; so could "Why MTV Is the Best TV Station." These topics are not suitable for research papers because both would be largely based on opinions rather than research.

Don't make the mistake of thinking that only things taught in school are worth writing about. Astronomy may not be taught in your school, but it's a subject that offers a lot of possibilities.

You may need to do some preliminary reading to help you choose your topic—to learn more about a subject, to see if the subject really interests you, to see how much has been published on the subject, and to see if it really is suitable for a term paper. Write down the titles and authors of any sources you consult.

REFINE YOUR TOPIC

Some Topics Are Too Broad

Chances are that your teacher's general topic or your own initial choice of topic will have to be narrowed down, or refined. "Whales" is too broad, as are "The Homeless," "Hispanic History," "African Americans," "Chemistry," and "Cars." Why bother narrowing your topic? Although these sound like perfectly good subjects, they will quickly get you into trouble.

- There is no way you can do a good job writing, say, a ten-page paper, or even a twenty-page one, on the general topic of whales. There is too much to say about whales, and you will end up with a superficial paper. At the very least, you would need to write an entire book to do justice to the subject!
- It's hard to do anything original with a vague topic such as "Whales" or "The Homeless" or

"Chemistry." All you will have is a vast collection of facts.

- Tackling a subject like "Whales" instead of one like "The Feeding Habits of the Blue Whale in the South Pacific" will require you to sift through too many references—you might find a hundred books and five hundred articles on whales. With a more specific topic, such as the feeding habits of one particular species of whale in one part of an ocean, you might do a good research job by reading only a few books and maybe a dozen articles.
- Organizing the information from hundreds of sources will be such an overwhelming task that you probably will never get around to writing the paper!
- Finally, most readers would rather learn a lot about a narrow topic than a little about a broad topic. With a broad topic, they will have a hard time grasping the facts you had a hard time trying to assemble.

Some Topics Are Too Narrow
A topic can also be too narrow. What is wrong with that? After all, less work is required. Here are the reasons against using a narrow topic:

- A topic that is too limited will lead to an overly specialized paper. Readers may be interested in the feeding habits of the blue whale, but unless they are marine biologists, they probably won't be interested in twenty pages on the migration habits of the blue whale's main food supply. However, if you are writing a research paper for a biology class, such a topic may be just what is required.
- If your topic is too narrow, you may be unable to find enough information—the opposite prob-

lem of too much information. No books may
exist on some extremely rarefied topics, and
the only articles available may be very specialized. These articles may be hard to understand
and hard to find and, just as your readers may
be bored by the migration patterns of krill, so
might you.

Making Choices

How do you tell whether a topic is too narrow or too
broad? For one thing, topics that are too broad sound
that way:
 History
 Drug Abuse
 Biology
 Sports
 Travel
 The Occult
 Immigrants

These could be, in some cases, whole fields of study.
When you go to the library and look up these topics in
the catalog or in the *Readers' Guide to Periodical Liter-
ature* (chapter 5 will help you with how to use library
resources), you may find too many sources cited—
such as a thousand articles on history, two hundred
books on sports, or eighty books on astrology alone!
You could narrow these topics down:
 The Civil War
 Alcoholism
 Trees
 Baseball
 Travel in China
 Astrology
 Asian-American Immigrants
  in the United States

Your topic may still be too vague: you uncovered eighty books on astrology, and you noticed tons of articles on baseball when you did your first search in the library. Even the Civil War may present a problem. How can you possibly describe the entire Civil War in ten pages, or twenty pages, or even a hundred? Try narrowing a step further:

> The Effects of the Civil War on Families in the North and in the South
> Is Alcoholism a Disease?
> The Effects of Acid Rain on Redwoods in Oregon
> A Comparison of the Pitching Styles of Dwight Gooden and Sandy Koufax
> Following the Silk Road through China
> The Role of Astrology in Hollywood Society
> A Comparison of the Lives of Vietnamese Immigrants in Texas Before and After the Vietnam War

We now seem to have more manageable topics.

Visit the library again and find out if too much information is available—or not enough. This involves checking the catalog of the library's holdings (the card catalog, or catalog on microfiche, in book form, or on-line), major periodical indexes, or CD-ROM systems, and maybe an on-line database, to get a rough idea of the quantity and types of sources that exist on your topic. You may be interested in knowing that an on-line service, such as the Bibliographic Retrieval System (BRS), might list hundreds or even thousands of articles on some topics.

Wait a minute. You have chosen the last topic listed, on Vietnamese immigrants in Texas, and find absolutely nothing on immigration before the Vietnam War. Your topic is too narrow, and you will have to rethink it.

With all topics, if the initial library work turns up too

*The "card" catalog—the key to the library—can
be available on cards, on microfiche, on-line
and accessed at computer terminals, or in
book form as seen here.*

many or too few sources, you will have to return to the drawing board to either refine or broaden the subject. Chapters 5 and 6 tell you more about the many different sources you will need for your research.

More Narrowing Techniques

Taking the broad topic of "The Homeless," there are several ways you can narrow it down.

Narrowing Topically

Homeless Senior Citizens
Homeless Shelters
Education for the Homeless
Food for the Homeless

Narrowing Chronologically

Homelessness During the Great Depression
Homelessness Before and After the Reagan
    Administration

Narrowing Geographically

Homelessness in New York City
Homelessness in Florida
Homelessness in Mexico

Combinations of Narrowing Techniques

Education for Homeless Children in New York
    City
Homelessness in Florida Before and After the
    Reagan Administration

Clustering or Webbing

With a general topic in mind, you can also narrow down your topic by a technique called "clustering" or "webbing." The first step is to take your broad topic and place it in the center of a page; place the main ideas about the subject as offshoots from the topic.

Select one of the offshoots to be the center of a new cluster.

Pick one or two areas that interest you and continue webbing and narrowing until you develop some possible research topics.

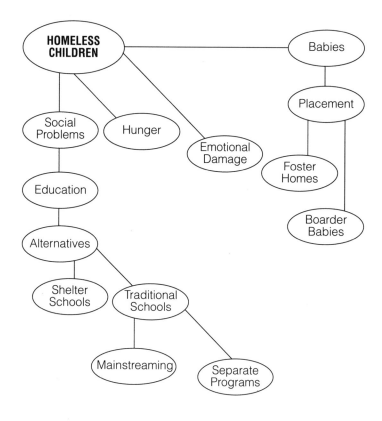

You might end up with:
> Alternatives to Traditional Schools for the Education of Homeless Children
> Mainstreaming Homeless Children
> Boarder Babies: An Approach to Nurturing Homeless Newborns

BRAINSTORMING

Another technique of choosing and refining a topic is brainstorming—letting your imagination run wild and writing down any topic that pops into your head, and then "creatively" refining. From a list of brainstormed topics, you eliminate those that seem farfetched or are too broad or too narrow. Creative refining can lead to a brilliant approach to your topic. Here are two examples:

1. You are assigned a research paper, but the choice of topic is all yours. You sit down, pen in hand, close your eyes, let your mind wander, and start jotting down all the ideas that come to mind, without thinking whether they are too broad, too narrow, or even appropriate for school: calligraphy, writing, models, model ships, sailing, vacations, cruises in the Caribbean, famous pirates, South America, Cortez, drugs in Colombia, jungles, cocaine, smuggling, police brutality, karate, wrestling, television, Madonna. . . .

2. You are assigned a general topic, such as "Science." You brainstorm as follows:
    The life of an eminent scientist
    Defending or disproving a scientific theory
    Describing in detail a plant, animal, element, planet
    Explaining how a certain scientific discovery has affected our lives
    Forecasting the shape of the future with the impact of certain discoveries

Although these ideas may be too broad or impractical, at least you have a place to begin. This technique is especially useful if you haven't the slightest idea of what you want to write about.

"HELP! I CAN'T THINK OF A TOPIC"

If you are stuck and can't think of anything to write about, don't give up. The world is a big place, you're smarter than you think, and school isn't that boring. There's got to be something for you to write about. Go to your teacher. That's right. Get up the courage to talk to your teacher about your problem. Probably your teacher will suggest a number of topics, or will gently try to get you to think of a topic on your own. Your teacher may ask you about your interests and subtly lead you to your very own idea.

You also can look through lists of suggested topics compiled especially for people in your shoes. One such book is *10,000 Ideas for Term Papers, Projects and Reports,* written by Kathryn Lamm and published by Arco (New York, 1991).

Another good source for ideas is the index volume of an encyclopedia. One encyclopedia includes the following entries under the heading "Greece, Ancient":

How Alexander spread Greek culture
Citizenship in ancient Greece
Funeral customs
Medicine
Advances in science
The Trojan War

Check other reference sources, too. *The New York Times Index* is a good one for news items; the *Scientific American* annual index may give you ideas for science reports. Thumb through current issues of your favorite magazines or of magazines related to your topic, if you were assigned one. As you skim, list topics or questions that interest you.

Another approach is to use a computer program such as the Americana Topic Finder and Research

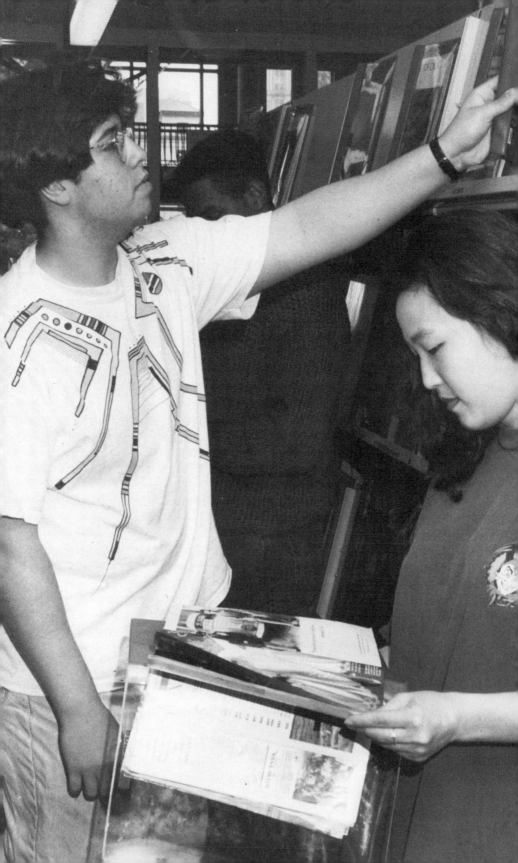

Planner. This software takes broad topics you are assigned, questions you about your own interests, and then provides a list of possible term-paper topics. This particular program even lists reference materials that contain the information you need.

And last but not least, talk to your school or public librarian. He or she has a lot of experience helping people with research papers—people just like you.

FINAL QUESTIONS TO ASK YOURSELF ABOUT YOUR TOPIC

1. Does this topic fit the assignment?
2. Is this topic researchable?
3. Do I have enough time to research this topic?
4. Can I find enough information?
5. Will this hold my interest?
6. Can I present this material effectively?

SUPER STRATEGIES

1. Think back to some topics that you studied in the course for which you are writing the paper. List the topics that immediately come to mind.
2. Skim your textbook and your notes for topics that interest you.

Current magazines might supply an idea for a term paper, or suggest a new way to approach a topic.

FOUR

A PLAN OF ATTACK: AN OUTLINE AND IDENTIFICATION OF KEY TERMS

THE OUTLINE

Once you feel secure and happy with your topic, write a one-paragraph summary of it. For instance, if your topic is "The Development of a Black Point of View in Art," your paragraph might be:

This paper will develop the idea that African-American artists have a special point of view related to being black. Six artists will be studied. Their descriptions of their work will be combined with my descriptions. I will show that each has been influenced strongly by upbringing, racial issues, color barriers, and "black consciousness."

A one-sentence statement, taken from the summary, which describes your entire paper is often called the "thesis statement." In this case, the first sentence, *This paper will develop the idea that African-American artists have a special point of view related to being black,* is the thesis statement.

You then need to flesh out this summary in anticipation of a serious attack on the library. A good way to do this is to construct a preliminary—or planning—outline. This needn't be a formal outline of the kind you have probably been learning to write since the fourth grade. All you have to do is jot down some ideas on your topic and put them in some kind of meaningful order.

You might like to sit by yourself in a quiet place, with a pad of paper and a pencil or pen ready, and close your eyes. (You should be a pro at this by now.) Visualize your topic: "Wyatt Earp," "Blue Whales," "Contemporary Women Artists," "The History of the Negro Baseball Leagues," "Education of Homeless Children in New York City," "Irony in the Writing of John Irving"—whatever.

Mull over the topic. Stretch it out. Look at one aspect of it. Visualize the baseball field, or the artwork, or the whales. Develop thoughts about aspects of your topic and follow these thoughts along main and side roads. What is most interesting about Wyatt Earp? His shooting ability? His strong friendships? Where and how did the first black baseball teams appear? How did the players' off-the-field hardships, in a segregated nation, affect their game?

You are developing your paper by "writing it in your head," before you know much about the subject. Because you have done little reading, you will be unable to do too much of this, but you can do enough to help you at least settle on an approach to the topic. As you turn up interesting thoughts, questions, conclusions, and avenues of discussion, jot them down. Let your mind wander over the topic in the same way it did when you were brainstorming about the topic.

Another strategy is to take a blank piece of paper and make two columns: "What I Already Know about

My Topic" and "What I Want to Find Out." For example, you may already know some things about the homeless children in New York City, such as: Some families are housed in welfare hotels; homeless children often miss school; and runaway children often become homeless.

From this, you can ask yourself some questions: Who are these homeless children? How many are there in New York City? Do all homeless children get some kind of education? How do they get to school?

Soon you will have several pages covered with notes. You can then sort through these notes, put them on index cards, or simply write them neatly on a fresh sheet of paper, or punch them into your computer, and set aside the material you have weeded out. Arrange the organized notes and questions in the order you think you'll want to use in your paper. Rough notes on your topic can later be turned into a more formal outline.

If you are unable to work in this fashion, you can simply do your thinking on paper, bypass the closed eyes stage, and just write down your ideas. Then select and organize them as before.

Whichever way you work, also make notes on possible illustrations, charts, graphs, or other material.

IDENTIFYING KEY TERMS

You will save a lot of time by further analyzing your topic and developing a plan of attack. Information in the library is arranged by subject, by time period, by

If you can't find a quiet spot at home to work out your planning outline, try the library.

geographical location, and by biographies of people involved. By reading a general encyclopedia article on your topic, you can note possible key terms to use to find information in the card catalog, periodical indexes, and other indexes. You should complete a list of 10 to 15 items, including key terms, the names of people, places, and events.

Topic: Education of Homeless Children in New York City

Key Terms: Homeless, Children, Education, New York City

Places: New York City, shelters, welfare hotels, skid row, schools

People: Activists for the homeless, including Mitch Snyder, Martin Sheen, Jack Kemp

Important Events: Reagan policies, HUD policies, McKinney Act

You are now ready to learn about the different reference materials you will use to help you prepare your preliminary bibliography.

SUPER STRATEGIES

1. Once you identify a few key terms from your thesis statement, check either the *Sears List of Headings* or the *Library of Congress Subject Headings* for related headings for books in the library. These volumes should be located near the library catalog.
2. Use the same procedure for periodical indexes with a "Thesaurus of Subject Headings" if available.

Key Terms	Synonyms	Broader Terms	Narrower Terms
homeless	Homelessness; street people	housing; poverty	homeless shelters; housing rehabilitation; welfare hotels; low-income housing; emergency shelters; runaways
education	schools; curriculum	culture; civilization	teachers; students; elementary education; secondary education; high schools; education—NYC; teaching; mainstreaming; socialization; busing; school buildings

FIVE

THE LIBRARY'S REFERENCE SOURCES

So much information is available today that many people call the time we live in the Information Age. The key to learning about one specific subject—without drowning in information—is to use reference sources.

Reference sources, such as the card catalog, encyclopedias, special books, and interviews, provide basic, concise information on your subject that will be invaluable when you start your preliminary reading. They also provide the names of more specific sources you will need when you compile your bibliography.

Where will you find the books, articles, pamphlets, maps, directories, cassettes, photographs, dictionaries, videotapes, and microfilm you need for your term paper? In the most important reference source of all: the library.

THE LIBRARY

Libraries tend to be laid out in different ways, but their materials are organized in pretty much the same manner.

The reference section of a large library offers a wide range of resources: encyclopedias, subject references, atlases, almanacs, and many more.

Reference materials, such as encyclopedias, almanacs, *Who's Who,* various directories, and "short histories," are usually found in one place. In a large library, this place will be large—occupying many shelves and rows. In a small library, these materials may be found in a few stacks of shelves. Reference books can sometimes be checked out for twenty-four hours in a school library, but usually must be used in the library. Such materials usually contain an R in front of the call number—R for Reference.

A card catalog will contain special cards telling you which books are contained in a particular library. Many libraries now have computerized "card" catalogs, and some put the card-catalog information in book form or on microfiche. Reference books are also listed in the card catalog. Bound periodicals are listed either in the catalog or on separate lists.

A reference room or area will have a *Readers' Guide to Periodical Literature* and perhaps an index to the *New York Times* (the newspaper with the motto "All the news that's fit to print"). These may be located near the card file or book catalogs.

Fiction is organized on the shelves by the last name of the author, not by call number. Biographies are organized by the last name of the subject, not the author. Nonfiction is organized by call numbers. There are two systems—the Library of Congress and the Dewey Decimal systems. Each has a different way for organizing nonfiction. You don't have to memorize these systems since in most libraries signs and labels direct you around the shelves.

Current magazines are usually on a rack; back issues, either loose or bound, are arranged on shelves. The same is true for newspapers, although back issues of the *New York Times* are found on reels of microfilm. Your library probably has a couple of microfilm readers, as well as microfiche readers. These may be in a sepa-

Using a microfiche reader

rate section. Microfiche are small cards of film containing reduced photographic images of magazines. As with reference materials, few libraries lend magazines and newspapers out and you will need to make photocopies.

Documents such as government publications and pamphlets are usually found on shelves or in drawers.

Since knowing your way around the library will save you a great deal of time, ask your teacher to take your class on a library tour or ask your librarian to show you around. Some libraries have brochures describing their layout, holdings, and use. A small library is easy to get to know, but a large library may be intimidating at first. Once you know where to look, you will be speeding around as if you own the place!

Some libraries today have computer systems that enable you to search the card catalog, magazine indexes, and perhaps encyclopedias and other reference books at a computer terminal. With some, you can retrieve the full magazine article right there. This "one-stop shopping" approach is becoming more and more common. The terminals may be in one spot or scattered through the library, especially if it is large. You may even be able to access the system from your home computer.

Now that you know where to locate the materials in your library, you will benefit from learning how to use them.

THE CARD CATALOG

The card catalog is often called the "key to the library," and for good reason. It is an index to nearly all of the materials to be found in that library. We are using the term *card catalog* in a general way, for a library's list of its holdings may be presented in a variety of forms.

Traditional card catalogs usually consist of a cabinet or cabinets with several drawers. The drawers are alphabetized, as are the cards inside the drawers. Many libraries have on-line catalogs, which are accessed by a computer terminal. Some libraries have book-type card catalogs; others use microfiche.

In addition to listing the library's holdings, the card catalog also tells you where the material is located. It does this by providing a call number for each book or periodical. All material in the library in turn is organized into groups with similar call numbers. Each catalog entry gives the call number (either numbers or letters or a combination of both). Once you match that number with the number of the book or periodical on the shelf, you are on your way.

Most card catalogs are centrally located in the library, although in large libraries you may find card catalogs in several locations.

Information can be accessed from the card catalog by subject, by author, and by title. Some libraries have totally separate catalogs for each of these categories.

Although the card catalog lists a number of kinds of sources, most people tend to use it to locate books. Let's look at a few examples of how to obtain information on a topic.

You have either decided to write on Iceland and are looking for a way to narrow your subject, or you have already settled on your final topic and are preparing your bibliography. You look in the card catalog under Iceland and find nothing listed. Don't give up yet. It is possible that you are looking in the wrong place. Because the card catalog follows a word-by-word method of alphabetizing instead of the letter-by-letter method used in dictionaries, Iceland appears after Ice Skating. Be careful you don't get thrown when you look up compound words.

It is possible that your library has no books on Iceland. But wait. Although no entire book may be

Using the library's on-line catalog

dedicated to the country of Iceland, information on Iceland might be available in other sources.

Iceland is part of Europe. Check the card catalog under Europe, find those books, and look in the index of each. No doubt you will find some information on Iceland. Similarly, if you can't find a whole book about the *Titanic,* look under Ships or Disasters. Books on alcoholism may be under Alcohol or Drug Abuse. Information on Wyatt Earp can probably be found in books about the Old West. Homeless shelters will most likely be covered in general books about Homelessness. This is where the list you have compiled of alternate subject headings becomes very useful.

Try to think of the broader picture and where your topic fits into it. Here are some examples:

Not Listed:	*Check:*
trout	fishes/fishing
pineapples	fruit/foods/Hawaii
Declaration of Independence	U.S. History/American Revolution
Buckingham Palace	England/Great Britain
Globe Theatre	Shakespeare
Oracles	Religion
Guns 'n Roses	Music—Rock
Arthur Ashe	Biography/Encyclopedia

Often the cards in the catalog will direct you to alternative subjects. These cards are called "see references" or "see also references" or "cross-references." When you look up Alcoholism, a card may say, "*See* Alcohol." Sifting through several cards on alcoholism may lead you to a card that says "*See also* Alcohol."

You also may want to search for a specific author. Perhaps you already know that Bruce Catton is a famous author of a number of books about the Civil War. You can look up "Catton, Bruce" in the card catalog to see if any of his books are in your library. Always look up names—whether they are names of authors or names of subjects—by the last name, first.

Another way to look up information is by title. Reference books can be looked up by title. (You may want to check to see which ones your library has before you actually head for the reference shelves.) If you are looking for a specific book—say, *The Sea Around Us*—you would do it by title. Disregard articles—*A, An,* and *The*—when they are the first word of a title, because so have the catalogers. To find *The Sea Around Us,* look under the letter S. *The Encyclopedia of Mammals* will be listed under E, not under T. Catalog cards give you a lot more information than the call number, subject, name of the author, and title. You can, for example, tell what the book is about, whether it contains photographs or illustrations, how long it is, and when it was published.

This information can be invaluable. If you are doing a report on computers and see that a book was published more than five years ago, you may want to skip it. If illustrations are a central part of your paper, you can tell which books have lots of illustrations and which have very few. The short summary on the catalog card will give you a feeling for the contents of the book. You also can obtain most of the information you need for your bibliography directly from the card catalog.

On-line catalogs work on much the same principle as regular card catalogs. However, instead of flipping through cards, you type in either the subject, name of the author, or title, on a keyboard, and the computer searches for references for you. The information then comes up on the screen. You can either write down

ALADIN

```
Search Request: A=TWAIN                          WRLC Libraries Catalog
Search Results: 742 Entries Found                           Author Guide
------------------------------------------------------------------ T7FA
LINE:   BEGINNING ENTRY:                                  INDEX RANGE:
  1     TWAIN DAVID 1929. CREATING CHANGE IN SOCIAL SETTINGS PLANN    1 -   53
  2     TWAIN MARK 1835-1910. ADVENTURES OF HUCKLEBERRY FINN TOM S   54 -  106
  3     TWAIN MARK 1835-1910. ART OF HUCKLEBERRY FINN TEXT SOURCES  107 -  159
  4     TWAIN MARK 1835-1910. CONNECTICUT YANKEE IN KING ARTHURS C  160 -  212
  5     TWAIN MARK 1835-1910. GILDED AGE A TALE OF TO DAY           213 -  265
  6     TWAIN MARK 1835-1910. LIFE ON THE MISSISSIPPI               266 -  318
  7     TWAIN MARK 1835-1910. MARK TWAIN SPEAKS FOR HIMSELF         319 -  371
  8     TWAIN MARK 1835-1910. MARK TWAINS MYSTERIOUS STRANGER MANU  372 -  424
  9     TWAIN MARK 1835-1910. ON THE POETRY OF MARK TWAIN           425 -  477
 10     TWAIN MARK 1835-1910. PUDDNHEAD WILSON AND THOSE EXTRAORDI  478 -  530
 11     TWAIN MARK 1835-1910. TRAMP ABROAD                         531 -  583
 12     TWAIN MARK 1835-1910. ADVENTURES OF HUCKLEBERRY FINN. TRUE  584 -  636
 13     TWAIN MARK 1835-1910. LIFE ON THE MISSISSIPPI SELECTIONS 1  637 -  689
 14     TWAIN MARK 1835-1910. SELECTIONS 1982. MISSISSIPPI WRITING  690 -  742
------------------------------------------------------------------
 STArt over        Type number to begin display within index range
 HELp
 OTHer options

 NEXT COMMAND:
ECHO                              CAPS                P.1 (024,016)
```

IF SCREEN IS OFF, PRESS "CLEAR" BUTTON

MLT7FA

*If you are researching Mark Twain,
for example, the on-line catalog
screen will display books
by and about the writer.*

what you need or, if the terminal is connected to a printer, print it out. An on-line system has many advantages over the traditional card catalog:

- The computer knows how the information is alphabetized.
- The computer will present all relevant material; it makes no distinction among titles, authors, or subjects. If you typed in "Albert Einstein," for example, you would see books by Einstein and about him, as well as books entitled *Albert Einstein*.
- Reponse time is quick.
- You may be able to see if a book has been checked out or is available.
- You may be able to access the information from home, if you have the equipment.
- You may be able to access the holdings of other libraries as well as your own.
- The computer automatically leads you to all the "see" and "see also" cards.

ENCYCLOPEDIAS

For some students, doing research means going to an encyclopedia and copying information from articles, word for word. This is plagiarism—literary theft—not research, and is totally unacceptable.

Other students, aware that copying an encyclopedia article is not the assignment, still mistakenly view the articles in encyclopedias as the complete and last word on the topic and use no other resources. This, too, is unacceptable. Encyclopedias give you an overview of your topic and help you find its major points and highlights. They are also helpful for looking up facts. The encyclopedia is a good starting point for research, but it definitely should not be the only source you use. The bibliographies at the end of the articles are also helpful as a starting point to lead you to other useful library sources.

The best way to extract information from an encyclopedia is to go to the index. If you check the index to research falcons, for example, you will find information on these birds in volumes other than the F one. Only by looking in the index would you know this.

Your library should have one or more of the following major encyclopedias:
Academic American Encyclopedia
Collier's Encyclopedia
Compton's Encyclopedia and Fact-Index
Encyclopedia Americana
Merit Student's Encyclopedia
The New Book of Knowledge
The New Encyclopedia Britannica
The New Standard Encyclopedia
The World Book Encyclopedia

Encyclopedias are also available in two different computer formats. These are on-line or CD-ROM. Some single-volume encyclopedias can also be stored on your computer's hard disk drive. With all these formats, you simply type in key words dealing with your topic and get back a list of relevant articles. You can then view the articles on a monitor or print them out. There is no need to look in several volumes for material on falcons, since the computer does it for you.

Going on-line means connecting your home computer to another computer over telephone lines. On-line encyclopedias can be used if you have a "modem," a device that enables your computer to "talk" over the telephone to computers at information services, called data banks. Some of the more popular services are BRS (Bibliographic Retrieval System), DIALOG, Prodigy, America Online, and CompuServe. Data banks store large amounts of information (called databases) in central computers. Prodigy and CompuServe are the most common for home use. BRS and DIALOG are used more by information specialists. A disadvantage of on-line encyclopedias is that you pay for each minute you use the computer, and the costs can quickly add up! A real advantage is that you can access this information twenty-four hours a day. Further, on-line encyclopedias are very up-to-date since new information can be added more quickly than it can in hardcover books.

CD-ROM (Compact Disc/Read-Only Memory) encyclopedias contain all the information that you would find in an entire set of encyclopedias, stored on a compact five-inch disc like the ones used for listening to music. A CD-ROM drive is needed to use CD-ROMs with a personal computer. The three most popular CD-ROM encyclopedias are *The New Grolier Multimedia Encyclopedia*, *Compton's Multimedia Encyclopedia*, and *Information Finder* (by World Book). Not only do these CD-ROMs enable you to search for text about your topic but they also display color photographs, illustrations, and sound and motion sequences.

An affordable alternative for the home-computer owner is an encyclopedia that can be loaded onto your hard drive. One example is *The Random House Encyclopedia*. Although not as comprehensive as either an on-line or CD-ROM encyclopedia (the material is taken from one single volume, rather than twenty or so separate volumes), this type of computer encyclopedia allows you unlimited searching at home for quick information, without the fees of on-line computers.

SUBJECT REFERENCE BOOKS

After your encyclopedia introduction to your topic, you may want to check for reference books devoted just to your topic. Every subject area has its special informa-

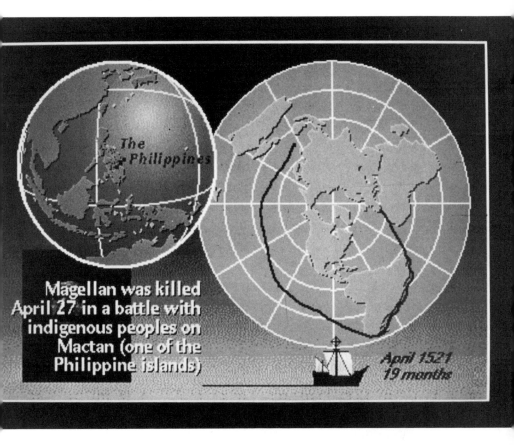

A screen from an encyclopedia on CD-ROM

tion sources. These books are useful and authoritative but like encyclopedias should be viewed only as starting points. Some provide overviews; others have excellent bibliographies. Many others are really only useful for finding and checking specialized facts.

OTHER GENERAL REFERENCE SOURCES

Almanacs contain a wide variety of information—especially statistics—updated yearly. These facts can be used to support statements in your report. You can find out who won the Academy Award for best actor in 1954, the results of presidential elections, the circulation of magazines, the addresses of associations, and so forth.

The *Statistical Abstract of the United States* is a handy tool. Most libraries keep it in the reference section. This book contains almost every kind of statistic about the United States, from the number of telephones to the number of people holding doctoral degrees. Such statistics can make your paper more interesting and authoritative. You may even be able to base your entire paper on statistics. You could use statistics about homeless children as the basis for a paper on education for homeless children.

Government documents and pamphlets are also useful. Libraries often store these in what is called the "vertical file." Sometimes these documents are indexed in the card catalog; sometimes they are not. If they are not, look up your topic in the vertical file, which will be organized alphabetically.

Many organizations such as the American Heart Association and the Dairy Council also publish pamphlets. In fact, you can pretty much assume that for all human activities or interests, there is an organization that disseminates information on the subject—whether it's building spaceships or building rubber frogs, fighting crime or fighting cockroaches. Every industry has a trade organization; every cause has organized advocates.

Here are some of the standard reference books on various subjects:

Animals and Plants

Atlas of Endangered Species
The Atlas of the Living World
The Audubon Society Encyclopedia of Animal Life
Audubon Society Field Guide series
The Encyclopedia of Aquatic Life
The Encyclopedia of Birds
The Encyclopedia of Mammals
Gray's Manual of Botany
Grzimek's Animal Life Encyclopedia
The Illustrated Encyclopedia of Birds of the World
The Illustrated Encyclopedia of Wildlife
The Marshall Cavendish Illustrated Encyclopedia of Plants and Earth Sciences
McGraw-Hill Encyclopedia of Science and Technology
Nature Atlas of America
The New Book of Popular Science
The Official World Wildlife Fund Guide to Endangered Species of North America
Oxford Companion to Animal Behavior
Peterson's Field Guide series
Simon and Schuster's Guide to Insects
Simon and Schuster's Guide to Mammals
Simon and Schuster's Guide to Trees
Walker's Mammals of the World

Earth and Space

The Cambridge Encyclopedia of Astronomy
The Facts on File Dictionary of Astronomy
The Facts on File Dictionary of Geology and Geophysics
A Field Guide to Rocks and Minerals
A Field Guide to the Stars and Planets
Magill's Survey of Science — Earth Science series
Magill's Survey of Science — Space Exploration series
The Marshall Cavendish Illustrated Encyclopedia of Plants and Earth Sciences
McGraw-Hill Dictionary of Earth Sciences
McGraw-Hill Encyclopedia of Astronomy
McGraw-Hill Encyclopedia of Geological Sciences
McGraw-Hill Encyclopedia of Science and Technology
McGraw-Hill Yearbook of Science and Technology
Space Almanac: Facts, Figures, Names, Dates, Places

Economics

Banking Terminology
Dictionary of Banking Terms
Dictionary of Insurance
The Dow Jones-Irwin Business and Investment Almanac
Encyclopedia of American Business History and Biography
Handbook of Labor Statistics
Handbook of Modern Accounting
Irwin Business and Investment Almanac
Manufacturing U.S.A.
McGraw-Hill Dictionary of Modern Economics

Occupational Outlook Handbook
Thomas' Register of Manufacturers
United States Business History, 1602–1988

Events/History
American Book of Days
Anniversaries and Holidays
Chronicle of America
Chronicle of the 20th Century
Chronicle of the World
Dictionary of American History
Dictionary of Historic Documents
Dictionary of the Middle Ages
Encyclopedia of the Third World
Encyclopedia of World History
Facts on File
Famous First Facts
Harper Encyclopedia of the Modern World
Harvard Guide to American History
Holidays and Anniversaries of the World
The New York Public Library Book of Chronologies
This Day in American History
This Fabulous Century
Time Lines on File
The Timetables of History

The Humanities
Benét's Reader's Encyclopedia of American Literature
Bulfinch's Mythology
Calendar of Literary Facts
Columbia Dictionary of Modern European Literature
Contemporary Literary Criticism
Contemporary Theatre, Film, and Television
Dictionary of Classical Mythology

Encyclopedia of World Literature of the 20th Century
The Facts on File Encyclopedia of World Mythology and Legend
Granger's Index to Poetry
The Great Song Thesaurus
The International Dictionary of Art and Artists
Macmillan Illustrated Encyclopedia of Myths and Legends
The Marshall Cavendish Illustrated History of Popular Music
McGraw-Hill Encyclopedia of World Drama
The New Arthurian Encyclopedia
New Grove Dictionary of Music and Musicians
New Harvard Dictionary of Music
New Oxford Companion to Music
Oxford Companion to American Literature
Oxford Companion series
Oxford Illustrated Encyclopedia of the Arts
Penguin Encyclopedia of Popular Music
Survey of Contemporary Literature

Ideas and Issues
The Dictionary of World Politics
Encyclopedia of Judaica
Encyclopedia of the Holocaust
Encyclopedia of Occultism and Parapsychology
Encyclopedia of Philosophy
Encyclopedia of Religion and Ethics
Encyclopedia of World Faiths

The reference area is often the busiest part of the library.

Facts on File Dictionary of Religions
International Encyclopedia of the Social Sciences
New Age Encyclopedia

Machines, Inventions, Technology

The Almanac of Science and Technology
Dictionary of Computing
Encyclopedia of Electronics
How it Works: The Illustrated Science and Invention Encyclopedia: Technology
Machinery's Handbook
McGraw-Hill Encyclopedia of Science and Technology
The New Book of Popular Science
The New Illustrated Science and Invention Encyclopedia
The Software Encyclopedia
Software Reviews on File
Van Nostrand's Scientific Encyclopedia
The Way Things Work: An Encyclopedia of Modern Technology
Yearbook of Science and the Future

People/Biography

Almanac of Famous People
American Writers
Asimov's Biographical Encyclopedia of Science and Technology
Baker's Biographical Dictionary of Musicians
Black Writers
British Writers
Contemporary Authors
Current Biography
Dictionary of American Biography
Dictionary of Literary Biography
Dictionary of Scientific Biography

Encyclopedia of Black America
European Authors
Facts about the Presidents
Great Lives from History
Index to Women of the World from Ancient to
    Modern Times
Lincoln Library of Sports Champions
The Lives of the Painters
The Lives of the Poets
McGraw-Hill Encyclopedia of World Biography
Men of Mathematics
Newsmakers
Notable American Women
Webster's American Biographies
Webster's Biographical Dictionary
Who's Who series

Places
Cities of the World
Encyclopedia of Historic Places
Facts About the States
Lands and Peoples
Maps on File
National Geographic Atlas of the World
New International Atlas
Rand McNally Goode's World Atlas
The Statesman's Year-Book World Gazetteer
Worldmark Encyclopedia of the Nations

Physics, Chemistry, and Medicine
American Medical Association Encyclopedia of
    Medicine
Black's Medical Dictionary
Concise Chemical and Technical Dictionary
The Consumer Health Information Source Book
CRC Handbook of Chemistry and Physics
Encyclopedia of Physics

Lange's Handbook of Chemistry
McGraw-Hill Encyclopedia of Physics
McGraw-Hill Encyclopedia of Science and Technology
Merck Manual of Diagnosis and Therapy
The New Book of Popular Science
The Oxford Companion to Medicine
Stedman's Medical Dictionary

PERIODICALS AND PERIODICAL INDEXES

Periodicals is just another name for magazines. They are called periodicals because they come out periodically—weekly, monthly, or at other intervals. Periodicals are useful or often essential for a variety of reasons:

- The information they contain is more current than that found in books or encyclopedias.
- They cover topics too new to have been covered in books.
- They cover familiar topics in new ways.
- They are a good source of pictures. BUT: DO NOT CUT UP PERIODICALS FOR THE PICTURES. MAKE PHOTOCOPIES.

How do you locate information in periodicals?

Let's suppose your report is on herbal medicine. In which periodical would you look? Would you consult the card catalog? Would you start paging through all the magazines in the library until you found some articles on herbal medicine? You wouldn't consult the card catalog, since articles are not indexed there. And looking through all the magazines in your library would take a long time. Even a small library subscribes to several dozen magazines and probably has back issues of other magazines as well. A large library may contain

Directories or indexes of periodicals
will lead you to articles with
up-to-date information.

hundreds of different periodicals. Thousands of periodicals of every imaginable kind are published in the United States.

Your job is made easy by indexes to the articles published in these periodicals. And the index to begin with, for almost all except very specialized topics, is the *Readers' Guide to Periodical Literature*—called the *Readers' Guide*, for short.

The *Readers' Guide*

The *Readers' Guide* takes some of the most popular magazines and lists the subjects covered in alphabetical order. It also indexes articles by author. However, 95 percent of the time you want to look something up, it will be by subject. The *Readers' Guide* does not index articles by title.

The *Guide* is published twice a month in September, October, December, March, April, and June, and monthly in January, February, May, July, August, and November. There are also quarterly and yearly compilations. The first few pages in the guide list the magazines indexed and explain all the abbreviations used.

To find listings for herbal medicine, you would first look under Medicine and also under Herbal Medicine. You might find titles and authors of articles, along with the name and date of the publication. You may also want to check other headings, such as Health, Herbs, and Healing.

How many volumes do you check? It all depends on the kind of information you are looking for. If you are writing on the use of medicinal herbs in the United States over the past ten years, you obviously will have to scour the *Readers' Guide* for ten years. If all you want is information on the medicinal use of herbs on communes in the 1960s, then probably checking the years 1960 through 1970 would be sufficient. If all you want is information on the herbs used by the president of France on a recent trip to China, all you would need would be the volumes just before, during, and just after the trip.

Since you will encounter many abbreviations in the entries, don't forget to look in the front of the *Guide* for any abbreviations you don't understand.

Although the *Readers' Guide* is an indispensable tool, it is doubtful that your school library will subscribe to all the magazines indexed, and, even then, it is not going to have every issue of the magazine ever published. Located close to the *Readers' Guide* should be a listing of which magazines the library owns and in which format they are held. Back issues may be loose, in bound volumes, or on microfilm or microfiche. Going through the *Readers' Guide,* finding pertinent articles, and determining whether or not they are available in your library, takes some time. You might have to go "back to the drawing board" several times to find available articles about your topic. If there is an article that you think you really can't do without, you may have to make a trip to a larger library unless your library participates in an interlibrary loan program. In that case, it is possible that another library will mail or fax the article to your school library.

Other Periodical Indexes

The *Readers' Guide* indexes only a percentage of the thousands of periodicals published in the United States. However, for many students, the *Guide* will be adequate most of the time. In cases where it isn't, you can consult some of the specialized periodical indexes that zero in on a particular field of study. The information indexed in these guides is much more technical than that found in the *Readers' Guide.* For instance, publications such as *Time* and *Newsweek* will be indexed in the *Readers' Guide* but not in the *Humanities Index.* On the other hand, articles in the *Bulletin of the*

Shakespeare Scholars of Tulsa, Oklahoma (if it exists) might be found in the *Humanities Index* but wouldn't be listed in the *Readers' Guide*. The special indexes are usually available only in larger school libraries and in public and college libraries. The actual periodicals will probably be available only in the larger libraries. Even then, you may have to go to microfilm for back issues. Here are some of the more widely used special indexes:

Applied Science & Technology Index
Art Index
Biography Index
Biological and Agricultural Index
Book Review Digest
Business Periodical Index
Cover Story Index
Education Index
General Science Index
Humanities Index
National Geographic Index
Scientific American Index
Social Sciences Index

When you go to the library, you probably will find several or many volumes of a particular index, arranged by date. Assuming you are not doing a historical survey, and just want recent information on a subject, start with the latest volume and work backward until you find what you are looking for. Just because what you are looking for isn't in one volume doesn't necessarily mean it won't be in another.

SIRS

SIRS stands for Social Issues Resources Series. These are large loose-leaf notebooks, each dealing with a different topic, that contain compilations of articles from newspapers and magazines. For example, there are SIRS volumes on Drugs, Pollution, Women, Mental Health, and other subjects. There is a cross-reference index to all volumes, as well as an index for each individual volume. SIRS are handy when doing research since the entire article is at your fingertips, and no additional "tracking down" is necessary.

There is also a CD-ROM version of SIRS. Here, you can type combinations of terms such as "homeless" and "education" and perform a search for related articles. Many of these can be printed in full length directly at the computer.

CD-ROM Periodical Indexes

If thumbing through years and years of back indexes to find periodical articles stresses you out, perhaps you are lucky enough to have access to a CD-ROM periodical index in your library. More and more high schools have them available. Some popular general ones are: *InfoTrac, Magazine Article Summaries,* and even a CD-ROM version of the *Readers' Guide.* It could be at its own station in the library, or you may be able to access it from the same terminal as the on-line catalog by switching menus.

On-Line Indexes

You were introduced to on-line indexes in chapter 3, in the description of how to access data banks to see how many articles were published on a topic. The real usefulness of these indexes is not in counting the numbers of articles, but in giving you the names and sources of these articles. Data banks such as DIALOG and BRS contain information about the sciences, medicine, business, social sciences, and marketing, as well as indexing government reports, and much more.

In on-line searching, you can type in keywords, and

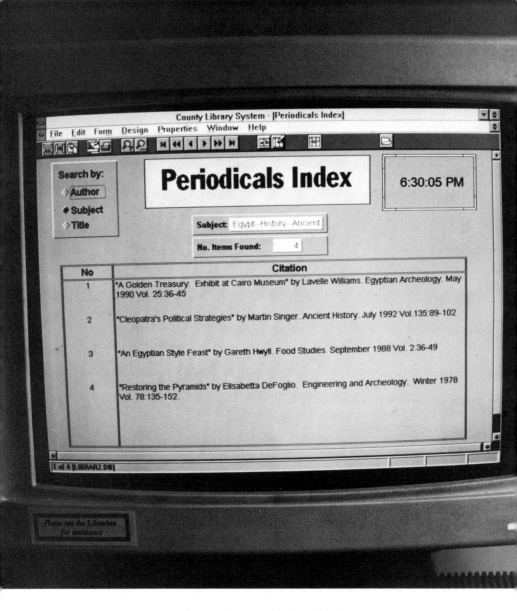

An on-line periodicals index

the computer will find all the articles that contain these words. It is necessary to choose these words carefully, or you will get a large number of irrelevant sources. At the same time, using the wrong words (or not using the right ones) could net you only some of the sources you need. These data banks are very up-to-date, and a search is done in a fraction of the time it would take for you to do it yourself.

For example, you need to find out how vitamin C affects the common cold. You could limit your search to articles published after 1990. You could search a database that has articles from popular magazines such as *Good Housekeeping* or *Time,* or you could search for articles in medical or scientific journals that doctors and scientists might use. Keywords might be vitamins, vitamin C, colds, viruses, and megavitamin therapy. If you have heard of Linus Pauling, who has done research on this subject, you could search for articles by or about him as well.

Because of the cost, on-line searching should be used only after all the traditional methods of searching out references have been exhausted. If you do conduct an on-line search, here are the steps to follow:

1. Identify the database or family of databases to be used—science, humanities, business, and so on.
2. List the keywords. If a thesaurus of keywords is available for your database, use it. Your search will be much more productive.
3. Decide if you want to limit your search by year(s).
4. Decide the type of information you want to receive: bibliography or bibliography and an abstract (a short summary of the article), or the entire article.

The information you get from an on-line search varies with the database used. For each article, most databases give the name of the author, the title, the name of the periodical, and an abstract. You will then have to take this information to the periodical section of the library and dig out the actual articles. The abstracts will help you determine whether the articles are worth reading. Sometimes the abstracts are lengthy enough for your purposes, and you won't need the full article.

You can read the abstracts on the monitor, which is an excellent way of finding out if you are going about your search in the right way. For instance, if all the abstracts you read about vitamin C and colds discuss only research on rats, you obviously need to add a keyword or words that indicate you want articles dealing with the effects on human beings (if that, indeed, is what you want).

More and more databases are becoming "full-text," meaning you can print out the entire article. If you have trouble accessing a large periodical collection, this is a good way to go. But even if your own library does not have a large periodical collection, it may have access to other libraries' collections through interlibrary loan. The articles may still take a while to get to your library, unless they can be faxed.

On-line searching is a powerful way to access information. Discuss its possibilities with your librarian or media specialist.

SUPER STRATEGIES

1. With an on-line card catalog you can often search by author, title, subject, or "keyword." By searching "keyword" instead of subject, you will find more information, and also be led to the correct subject heading to search.

2. Once you locate information under a certain call number in the stacks, check the reference section under the same call number for additional information.
3. A local computer club, computer store, or university computer center will often have lists of phone numbers that allow free access to libraries' data banks in your area via modem.
4. *America Online* includes a "teacher pager," which works something like a police all-points bulletin, for research help. Students can post questions and receive answers from a database of several hundred teachers.

SIX

PRIMARY SOURCES

There are two main kinds of research sources: primary and secondary. Primary sources are the original writings of authors: novels, nonfiction books, articles, poems, diaries, or letters. Interviews, oral accounts, photographs, and real objects from the past are also primary sources. Government documents, such as compilations of unemployment figures of the *Congressional Record,* are primary sources, as are transcripts of speeches.

Secondary sources interpret, analyze, paraphrase, and report information contained in primary sources. Secondary sources can be located through the library catalog and other resources listed in the previous chapter.

For example, while writing on the early development of rock and roll music, you will want to go to both primary and secondary sources. You would read the lyrics of Chuck Berry songs, listen to Buddy Holly's songs, watch videos of performances, and read interviews with Elvis Presley (all primary sources); and you would read critics such as Robert Christgau and historical surveys (secondary sources).

Can you be expected to track down, read, and understand a bunch of old speeches, thousand-page volumes of boring statistics, collections of letters written in French, scientific papers obviously directed at geniuses, and moldy out-of-print books your library probably wouldn't have? No, but when possible, *try* to look at primary sources. In fact, you may have to. You may also find them to be exciting reading.

Let's say one book you are reading mentions another book, by the "leading expert on whale food." You really will have to find this book, if you don't have it on your list already. Why read about this expert's work secondhand when you can get it from the horse's mouth?

Primary sources can also make your report unique and much more interesting. It is one thing to string together a collection of facts about how homeless children are educated, but quite another to spend a few hours observing them in a classroom or interviewing teachers.

HOW TO LOCATE PRIMARY SOURCE MATERIAL

Some of the primary sources mentioned may be found in your school library—diaries, speeches, letters, and books. In addition, your library may have some photographs, slides, or videotape footage.

The public library could have a more extensive primary source collection, including taped interviews, called "oral histories," and old newspapers either in the original form or on microfilm. Both your school and the public library may have a "community resource file," a listing of experts who live in your area and are willing to share their knowledge. Community resource files are found in card files, file cabinets, loose-leaf binders, or even as an option on some on-line card catalogs. Ask local librarians if they know of a community resource file for your area. It may be located at the Chamber of Commerce office.

Objects from the past are primary sources,
often providing fascinating information that
can be incorporated into other research.

Besides libraries, there are many other ways to access primary source material. Contact local historical societies, newspaper offices, galleries, museums, historic sites, government agencies, universities, and one of the best primary sources—people.

These institutions or people can be located through the community resource file—the Yellow Pages— under "collectors," through newspaper articles touting their accomplishments, or through word of mouth. Interviews with experts can be valuable. Not only will they give you an uncommon perspective but they may also be able to help you refine your topic, check your facts, and organize your material. Naturally, you don't expect anyone else to write the paper for you, but general recommendations and fact checking won't hurt.

Members of your own family are great resources. They may be "experts" in their own right. A grandparent will be able to tell you a lot about how lifestyles have changed in your community since cable TV; an uncle who served in Vietnam will be able to add depth to your report about the war.

INCORPORATING PRIMARY SOURCE MATERIAL

The primary sources you use should support your thesis. For example, you may wish to show that classrooms in homeless shelters are inferior to those in suburban schools. You could take several photographs of each, to compare crowding, materials available, cheerfulness of the rooms, as well as other details. Examinations of the works of black artists may, or may not, support the hypothesis that there is such a thing as "black art."

A NOTE ABOUT COURTESY

Special permission is often needed to use historical documents or collections. Be sure to make a courteous

HOLOCAUST
LIBRARY

This equipment
for use with
Holocaust Materials
only!
Your cooperation
is appreciated.

phone call or write a letter beforehand to set up an appointment that is convenient to the host agency. Be very careful when handling the materials.

If you are conducting an interview, come prepared with a list of questions. Include both specific questions, "How many homeless children go to school here?" and open-ended questions, "What makes teaching homeless children rewarding?" Listen carefully to the person's responses and don't interrupt. If you want to tape the interview, ask permission before you start. If you aren't recording, take accurate notes. Thank the person at the end of the interview, and follow up with a thank-you note or letter. The same set of rules applies to phone interviews.

Make sure you cite interviews, or other primary source material, in your footnotes and bibliography. When citing interviews, note the time and place where they were conducted.

SUPER STRATEGIES

1. A large number of primary source materials, especially photographs and documents, have been reproduced and stored on video-discs. These can be accessed via computer. Extensive indexes may accompany these discs, allowing quick access to specific bits of information.
2. It may be difficult to decipher primary source material. Keep a magnifying glass and a dictionary handy while you are reading.

Students view videotaped primary source material in a library's special collection.

SEVEN

ℐHE WORKING BIBLIOGRAPHY

Now that you know something about different types of sources, it is time to put together a working bibliography. The working bibliography consists of all the sources you think you will use for your research. It is a "working" bibliography because, as you do your research, you will be uncovering new sources to add to this bibliography. And when you finish doing your research, you will undoubtedly find that you have not used a number of the items listed in the original bibliography. By the time you have actually finished writing the paper and are compiling the final bibliography, you probably will find that your initial list has changed considerably.

HOW TO BUILD A BIBLIOGRAPHY

To build a bibliography, you will have to consult the various references discussed in the previous chapters. The only information you should be gathering at this point is the names of books, articles, videotapes, pamphlets, and other documents about your subject.

Start with a visit to your librarian. Mention sources you have already checked or plan to check. Your librarian probably can suggest others.

Check the card catalog for titles of books. Go to an encyclopedia. If you look at the end of many of the articles, you will find a reading list. Some of these sources may prove useful. Also consult short histories, "concise guides," and books listed in chapter 5.

Look in bibliographies on your topic; these may list tens or hundreds of books and articles. Critical bibliographies will give you useful points on books on the subject. For example, these would be listed in the card catalog under "Homeless— Bibliography." Books published especially for students may contain useful bibliographies, perhaps of easy-to-understand books and articles. Two such series of books are *The Reference Shelf* by the H.W. Wilson Company, and *Opposing Viewpoints,* by Greenhaven Press. You can access these series in most card catalogs. Just look up *Reference Shelf* or *Opposing Viewpoints*, and you should find cards for those topics that are available.

Check the periodical guides and on-line data bases for titles of relevant articles. Find pamphlets.

Jot down names of people you might want to interview or places you might want to visit.

LIMIT THE SIZE OF YOUR BIBLIOGRAPHY

Three factors will automatically limit the number of sources you include in your bibliography: the amount of time you have to complete the assignment, the usefulness of the source because of the level at which it is written or the language it is written in, and the availability of the source.

Because your time is limited, you probably cannot read all the books and articles you find on your topic— unless there is very little available information. Furthermore, at least some of the materials will be too difficult or technical, or in a language you do not understand. Some of the materials will be unavailable, even in the larger libraries near your home.

Two principles will help you make the best use of your time and find the most valuable sources.

First, find the best authors in the field. In every subject area there are recognized authorities, from astrology to rap music to capital punishment. Take note of names of authors or titles of books that turn up again and again; read critical bibliographies and bibliographies in textbooks; talk to your teacher or to experts in the field. There is no need, for example, to read all the biographies of John Lennon—only the best ones.

Second, try to use the most recent books and articles. In a field such as astronomy, where there are hundreds of general books, and where theories seem to be modified monthly, you will want to choose only the most recent books for your paper on quasars. The recent books will incorporate all the earlier material, anyway. However, you still may want to read the first accounts of quasars written by their discoverers.

Should you be counting the number of sources used? Do you have to include materials from each type of source? The answer is no in both cases, but it is important to include the best sources, from scholarly books to popular articles. Books are comprehensive but less up-to-date than articles. Articles are often more important than books, especially in science and for social issues.

Choose secondary sources carefully. If you are writing about the life and works of Alice Walker, the American fiction writer, you will want to include biographies and works of criticism (secondary sources), as well as her own writings. In the case of an author such as Shakespeare, about whom thousands of books have been written, you will have to be selective or you will be reading for the rest of your life.

COMPILING THE BIBLIOGRAPHY

A good way to compile your list of references is to enter them on 3-by-5-inch index cards.

Each card should contain the name of the author or authors, title of the article or book, date of publication, place of publication (for a book), and name of publisher (for a book). A magazine or encyclopedia article should also include the volume and page numbers. The information should be complete and in the same form you will be using when you compile your final bibliography. Chapter 11 will help you with this.

Also, include the library catalog number for a book, or a note on the location of the reference in the library. This will enable you to go straight to the reference when you are ready to start your reading. Arrange the cards alphabetically, by the author's last name. Number each card in one corner—1, 2, 3, and so forth. Later, you will be able to refer to the source by number on your research note cards, saving you a great deal of time and possible writer's cramp.

USING A COMPUTER

You also could use a computer to build your list of sources. This can be done in several ways. A general database program would enable you to set up a format for computer "cards." Your database would include the same information as the cards, using author as a *field*, title as a *field*, and so on. Then, once you were finished, the computer could be given instructions to print out the bibliography according to your format. The same information in the database would be available to be printed out as references (if they are to appear at the end of the paper). You could also include a field for notes for the actual information you use later.

Pro-Cite (Personal Bibliographic Software) is a software program for IBM and Macintosh computers that deals specifically with bibliographies. The database fields are already constructed, and you simply input the information. This program has the ability to print out your bibliography in any of the acceptable styles, such as that recommended by the Modern Language Association or by Turabian, in *A Manual for Writers of Term Papers, Theses, and Dissertations*.

There are also programs specifically for writers of term papers. Term Paper Writer (Activision) and Research Paper Writer (Tom Snyder Productions) have modules, or sections, for taking notes, outlining, and printing bibliographies.

Using a computer allows you to add and delete materials as your bibliography evolves, and you do not have to retype it each time. So, you can spend more time working on the writing, rather than the mechanics, of your paper.

Many people today have portable computers that they take directly to the library. Here they can input the information right on the spot, which saves even more time.

SUPER STRATEGIES

1. Include a field for "name of library" in your database. You can later sort your list of potential sources by library, saving time when you return for more information.
2. If you've never used a computer before, don't start with an entire term paper as your first project. There will be too much pressure. Learn smaller tasks first, such as writing and editing paragraphs, and inputing information into a database.

EIGHT

THE OUTLINE

Once you have assembled a working bibliography, you will need to do some more reading so that you can write a more complete outline. Reading in some of the better books on your subject will help you now.

Most authors, whether of novels, magazine articles, biographies, scholarly papers, or books, make an outline of what they plan to include in their writing. Many teachers require students to construct outlines before writing term papers. Often the outline must be turned in along with note cards, the working bibliography, rough drafts, and the final paper.

Some people believe that an outline should be very detailed, moving along paragraph by paragraph, with topics, subtopics, and sub-subtopics. Others believe outlines ought to be only as detailed as one needs so that key ideas are not forgotten.

There is no guarantee that doing an outline will automatically lead to a great paper. However, if you haven't written many research papers, feel a little nervous about the process, or have a hard time organizing your material, then consider a fairly detailed outline as a requirement—whether or not your teacher makes it one. In case your teacher does not give you an outline format, here's one you might try.

First, break up your topic into large pieces. Pretend, for instance, that you are writing a book on your topic and are thinking up chapter divisions. Make a list of these. A computer will come in handy, since you can easily modify the list by changing the entries, inserting new ones, and rearranging them. You may have something like this:

> The reasons why children are homeless in today's society
> Education of homeless children
> A description of each type of education solution
> Comparisons of each solution
> Problems homeless children face getting an education
> The best ways to educate homeless children

TIGHTEN YOUR FOCUS

You can approach the theme of the education of homeless children in a variety of ways.

For instance, perhaps you want to begin the outline with the question: What is the best way to educate homeless children? You will need to describe the alternative methods and compare them. For each solution, you will need to discuss:

> Costs
> Traveling time and distance
> Outside support required

As library technology continues to improve, researchers gain easier access to many information sources.

How the homeless students fit in with the school community
What advocates say about this method
What critics say about this method
What the homeless children say about this method

You can insert this list under the appropriate general "chapter" in your outline. You may number the chapters or simply use line breaks, indents, underlining, or bold-face type to mark the distinctions. The outline below may be what you're used to doing.

   I. Short history of education for homeless children
  II. Educational solution 1
     A. Definition/description
     B. Costs
     C. Travel time required
     D. Outside support required
     E. How homeless students fit in the school community
     F. Views and opinions
       1. Advocates
       2. Critics
       3. What homeless children say

  III. Educational solution 2 (etc.)

Once you have an outline, you probably will want to flesh it out even more and perhaps add a few little notes:
    How homeless children fit in the school community:
      Discuss whether or not students have a separate classroom

Give examples of elementary and secondary students
Mention school lunches

You also may want to indicate the amount of space you
think you'll want to give to each point:
How homeless children fit in (250 words)
or:
How homeless children fit in:
Comparison of elementary and secondary
schools (two paragraphs)
School lunches (short paragraph)

You can map out your paper paragraph by paragraph,
but this may be more detailed than you need. It may
prevent you from developing your own personal writing
style, and may make the final paper sound like a suc-
cession of disconnected paragraphs. It may also take
the fun out of writing and inhibit you from thinking as
you write. Most writers develop their ideas as they
write; they don't just fill in the blanks.

OUTLINE ALTERNATIVES

There are other alternatives to the traditional outline
that you may have used in the past or may feel more
comfortable with.

One method calls for writing each of your key ideas
on an index card. Using the example of education for
homeless children, you would have one card that says
"costs" on it, another with "critics," and so on. These
cards could be arranged and rearranged on a flat
surface until you determine a sequence you like.

A cluster, or web map, allows you to visualize rela-
tionships in your data. (See example on page 84.)

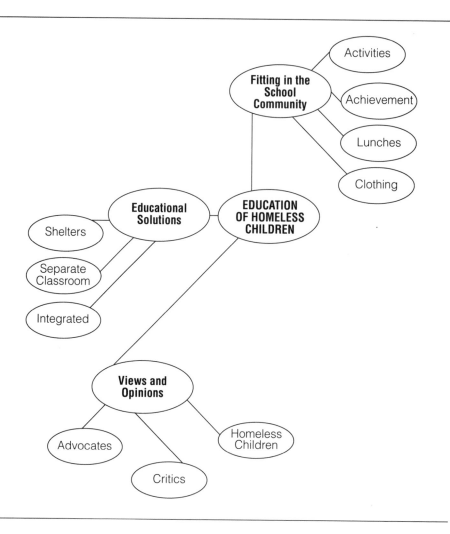

Some students may prefer a simple chart to an outline.

Education of Homeless Children

Educational Solutions	Views and Opinions	Fitting in the School Community
Shelters	Advocates	Activities
Separate	Critics	Lunches
Classroom	Homeless	Achievement
Integrated	Children	Clothing

Once again, your instructor may want something different, or you may have worked differently in the past and want to do this outline the way you have done all others. Just keep in mind that an outline is simply a tool to help you write a better report.

ANOTHER LIBRARY VISIT

After developing your outline, you may realize that you need more information to support your thesis. If this is the case, go back to the library for more information.

SUPER STRATEGIES

1. Think only of main ideas as you are composing your outline. Don't get bogged down worrying about grammar, punctuation, transitions, or other small details at this stage.
2. Exchange two or three versions of your outline with a friend or group of friends. Discuss which one makes the best sense.

NINE
TAKING NOTES

Once you have located the sources you intend to use for your research and have prepared your outline to guide you, it is time to go through the sources and take notes.

HOW TO READ, WHAT TO NOTE

Take notes as you read. Do not read and try to make notes later on from memory. Approach each source with your topic clearly in mind and know exactly what you want from that source.

If you are writing on Mitch Snyder, homeless advocate, and have selected two book-length biographies and ten articles on his social contributions, you may be able to derive all the necessary biographical information from the books and can ignore the biographical information in the articles—unless the books do not cover it.

While studying the sources, you may notice much of the same material—especially if you're using biographies and popular articles. Once you take down a

Take notes as you read. Most researchers find index cards easier to work with than a notebook, but the most important point is that you record the information and the source when you find it.

piece of information from source A, there is no need to note it again from source B—unless it is a surprising item and you wish to note a corroborating source.

Read slowly, and note only information pertinent to your topic. This usually requires a lot of sifting. For example, you may read a long article on the homeless and find only one sentence of value. Another book may yield fifty pieces of information. Refer back to your outline and your research questions to help you recall what you really want to know.

As you read, you may come across conflicting information. One book says your subject was born in France; another says it was Germany. You may also find points you aren't sure of or can't find answers to, or you may wonder about some aspect of your topic. Jot down these notes and questions on note sheets or cards, perhaps of a different color from those you've been using to collect information, or put a symbol in one corner, perhaps a question mark, or the word NOTE or QUESTION. As you read further, the answers may pop up. If they don't, additional research will be necessary.

TAKE NOTES ON CARDS OR ON A COMPUTER

Unless your teacher specifies otherwise, take notes on 3-by-5- or 4-by-6-inch cards. (Some people prefer using sheets of paper of this size instead.)

Do not make notes in books or tear out pages of books or magazines. You may photocopy materials in the library if you prefer doing some of your note taking at home. You may want to make copies of key articles, helpful reading lists, or even an especially useful chapter for quick reference.

You also can take notes on a computer, using a database program. Database programs have many names: filing programs, database managers, indexers, notebook programs. They should be able to handle a large amount of information, break it down into several categories (called fields), sort it by these fields, and then print it out.

Once the fields are set up, you fill them in, one by one, with the information you collect. The database programs will allow you to view the contents of the note cards on the screen and then sort the note cards by field, and then print them out. You can use your database program to print out your information in different arrangements, too. For example, you can construct and alphabetize your sources by the author's last name, or group together information of a similar nature.

You may want to try special computer software such as Term Paper Writer (published by Personal Choice Software, Mountain View, Calif.), which contains a word processing program and can also help you take notes, prepare an outline, and compile your footnotes and bibliography.

TAKE NOTES SYSTEMATICALLY

Write the number of the reference in one corner of the card. If you don't want to use numbers, use an abbreviated title of the work instead:

Gibbon, The Decline and Fall of the Roman Empire, volume 8
or
Decline & Fall, vol. 8
or
Gibbon, vol. 8

Put down one fact, or group of closely related facts or main ideas on each card. This way you can easily organize your information when you write the paper. You will be able to organize the cards quickly, weed out duplicate material, and discard and insert material without having to hunt through a lot of unnecessary scribbling.

You might write the definition of oceanography on one card, the names of its six pioneers on another card, one main achievement of each pioneer on each of six cards, and so forth. When writing the paper, you may want to use only three achievements, so you can put aside the other three cards. Had you put all this information on one card, you would have had a lot more work to do while separating the useful from the useless information. It also is easier to jot down just a few words at a time on one card than many sentences.

Add to each card the page number or numbers of where the information appeared in each source, even if you are neither paraphrasing nor quoting material. This makes it easy to go back and check your facts, add material, and document borrowed ideas.

Give each card a topic code as you go along. For instance, in your research on whales, you might decide on five sections: whaling, whaling operations, economics of whaling today, the morality of whaling, and the activities of Greenpeace and other organizations opposed to whaling. As you go through a reference and find information on one of these topics, you would code the information as History, Operations, Economics, Morality, or GP. The code would go in a blank corner of your note card, perhaps circled.

Write legibly. If you don't, you will get the facts wrong later, or may have to re-research some of the information. Using abbreviations is okay, as long as you can decipher them later. Note your abbreviations on a card or piece of paper.

Why code your cards? Because when you finish going through your references, you can easily sort the cards according to the topic codes, then organize them until you achieve the order you want.

When you finish taking notes from one source, whether you make only a few notes or one hundred, put a rubber band around the card or cards and place a card on top indicating the reference source. That way you know which pile is which.

EVALUATING INFORMATION

Not everything you locate on your topic will be accurate, factual information. Writers are only human, and sometimes they make mistakes. You will be more likely to discover factual mistakes in newspapers or magazines than in books. Or, sometimes, writers' attitudes, values, or personal experiences will affect the way they present information.

How can you tell which information is accurate and factual and which might be opinions or value judgments? Recognizing provable statements is usually easy in scholarly materials because footnotes, in-text references, and bibliographies lead readers to the writer's proof. Here are some other clues that signal facts, as opposed to opinions or personal values.

Facts: use of active verbs; present and past tenses of "to be" verbs (is, was, has been); statistics; specific details that can be proved true or false.

Opinions: use of subjective verb forms (could, might, would); verbs expressing opinion (believe, think, assume); qualifiers (probably, maybe, almost, perhaps); hypothetical situations (if . . .); predictions of future events (will, ought to); adjective qualifiers (fine, unnecessary, scandalous).

Values: inclusion of judgments from good to bad; comparisons (sweetest, nicer, happier).
(This section on evaluating information was adapted from *Brainstorms and Blueprints,* by Barbara K. Stripling and Judy M. Pitts, Englewood, Colo.: Libraries Unlimited, 1988.)

Activist organizations publish books and pamphlets to circulate their points of view. You will get very different perspectives on whales from the environmental group Greenpeace than you will from, say, a fishing organization representing people trying to make a living from whale products. If you are unsure about the political stance of a group or writer, ask for help from your teacher or library media specialist.

ACKNOWLEDGE OTHER PEOPLE'S IDEAS

There is a right way to extract information from a source—and a wrong way.

The right way is to either take notes in your own words, or quote any material you are taking directly from the author. If your wording is close to that of the author, use quotes but make a note on the card saying "paraphrase." To paraphrase is to put someone else's ideas into your own words. Put quotations or paraphrases on note cards in the same way that you recorded other information, discussed earlier. Indicating the page number(s) is essential.

When the time comes to turn your notes into paragraphs, you will cite, in footnotes or notes at the end of your paper, the sources of ideas, even if you express these ideas in your own words.

Not giving credit where credit is due is *plagiarism.*

Plagiarism is against the law. It is cheating, and it is unethical. It ignores the basic idea that students should do their own work. In college, plagiarism may lead to expulsion from school. Even if you do not deliberately steal from another author, you may be accused of plagiarism if you use someone else's wording or ideas without giving that person due credit.

When and How to Paraphrase
or Use Quotations

Use quotations sparingly. They are especially useful (1) when the author says something so effectively or beautifully that you want to capture the language of the original, (2) to lend authority on the subject, and (3) in a critical paper, where you discuss someone else's writing.

Paraphrasing is handy when you want to condense someone's important ideas or add a touch of authority to your paper. Here is a passage from an imaginary book by an imaginary social critic, E. M. Short:

> *Society as a whole should take responsibility for the homeless, rather than blame them and then incarcerate them. Is it their fault that they were born into poverty, or were victims of discrimination, or were simply unable to cope with unemployment and too large families? No, of course not. Society must assume much of the blame for their lot and correct their lot rather than punish the victims.*

Here is your paraphrase on the note card:

> *Short would put much of the blame for homelessness on society rather than on the individuals themselves, whom he sees as victims.*

The paraphrase is brief. It summarizes Short's views. It is in the paraphraser's own words. It is not just the original quotation with a few words changed, or the sentence order reversed. The paraphraser has understood Short's meaning, then restated it.

TAKE NOTES ON POSSIBLE ILLUSTRATIONS

If you see charts, tables, photographs, diagrams, cartoons, or drawings you may want to include in your paper, note their sources in the same way you have been recording other information. You will need to credit these sources when the time comes.

Type of Information	Type of Note
General explanatory material	Summary
Supporting information	Paraphrase
Examples	
Causes	
Effects	
Comparison/Contrasts	
Proof	
Arguments	
Specific details	Citation
Definitions	
Statistics	
Predictions/conclusions/hypotheses	Paraphrase
Biographical information	Paraphrase
Primary source information	Quotation

This information on guidelines for note taking was adapted from *Brainstorms and Blueprints*, by Barbara K. Stripling and Judy M. Pitts, Englewood, Colo.: Libraries Unlimited, 1988.

SUPER STRATEGIES

1. Eliminate multiple secondary sources of the same information by checking publication dates and using only the most recent ones.
2. Generally speaking, books that have extensive bibliographies and footnotes are more authoritative sources.
3. Certain authors and publishers are considered experts in specific fields. Check with your library media specialist about possibilities for your topic.

TEN

A LITTLE LECTURE ON WRITING

Before you begin the actual writing of your paper, you might benefit from a short lecture on writing. It is a "little" lecture because everyone hates lectures, especially long ones.

After speaking, writing is the most important form of communication in our society. Everywhere we turn, we see words in print, from the writing on gum wrappers, cereal boxes, and television commercials, to books and newspapers. In doing your term paper, you are joining the ranks of all those writers contributing to the enormous flood of written and printed words overwhelming our daily lives.

Even though your paper is an assignment for school and your topic may be of little interest to anyone but yourself and your teacher, why not imagine you are writing for a wider audience? Why not imagine you will send your paper to a popular magazine or to a scholarly journal, or that you will read it in front of an audience composed of your fellow students, or perhaps composed of people from college admissions offices?

In other words, since you are going to work to dig up facts and organize them into something meaningful, why not also put some energy into the way you express yourself? While it is true that, except in English class, a decently written, well-organized, and well-thought-out term paper will be enough to get you a good grade, a paper that is also well written may snare you the more prized A or A+. That is because teachers (and other readers) appreciate good writing, and often associate good writing with good organization.

Writing well requires effort and practice so let's spend just a little time looking at some of the characteristics of good writing and some of the things to consider while you complete your term paper.

AUDIENCE

Each audience is different: soap-opera lovers watching commercials, match-cover perusers, readers of *Time* magazine or of the *National Enquirer,* or of Shakespeare or Christopher Pike, of shampoo labels and instructions for using computer software. As a writer, you have to consider your audience and write for it.

In your case, the main audience is your teacher. However, if you think only of your teacher, the result will be very narrow, too private. Think of your teacher as being part of a larger audience composed of intelligent readers. Their degree of sophistication depends in part on the subject. While your teacher may know something about your topic, it is better to pretend that he or she doesn't. This will prevent you from skipping over the basics of your topic or becoming too specialized. By assuming intelligence, you will avoid being too simplistic.

For example, in writing a paper on whales for a biology class, you can assume that your teacher understands the general principles of biology and knows a little about a lot of animals. You can also assume that your teacher probably knows little about whales. You needn't define migration, but you will need to discuss the specifics of whale migration.

STYLE AND TONE

The consideration of your audience will affect your style and tone.

Since you are not writing for whale experts, you shouldn't adopt the remote, formal, stilted, dry tone you might see when one specialist writes for other specialists. You can find this kind of writing in professional journals. Although precise language is always welcome, the specialists are as bored by the writing of these articles as you or your teacher would be reading them. The difference is that they *have* to read the articles to keep up with developments in the field; if the article is well written, perhaps even a little entertaining—fine; if it's not, well, that's to be expected.

Conversely, too informal a style and too friendly a tone are inappropriate for the conveyance of hard scientific facts. Since your teacher is like a reader of a magazine like *Time* or *Science News,* or of a general-interest history publication, it is appropriate to be somewhat relaxed and even to allow yourself some humor or other flights of the imagination. This is especially appropriate with a paper on a literary figure or work, where good writing is valued more than in the sciences. Injecting a joke into a science report is probably unacceptable, unless the joke fits in with the purpose of the experiment.

Avoid jargon, even in technical writing. Jargon is a collection of specialized terms used by practitioners of certain disciplines. While jargon serves as a helpful shorthand, its use has led to the enormous gap that now exists between the general public and the specialists in various fields, and even between specialists in different branches of the same field! Neuropsychologists are no longer always understood by neurosurgeons or by behavioral psychologists!

LANGUAGE

Words are the building blocks of writing. How they are used is obviously what determines the way your ideas will be received. While dry writing is boring, flowery language—using a lot of modifiers—is equally offensive. As usual, the middle ground often is the most successful.

> *Plants inhabiting the littoral zone often extrude themselves onto composites, thirty to sixty feet from the next zone.*

> *A myriad of extraordinarily lovely and breathtakingly colorful plants that have spent years establishing their homeland in the magical zone between high and low tides remarkably often creep longingly onto the bric-a-brac of massive boulders a mere thirty to sixty feet from the zone of conifers and other symmetrical organisms.*

> *Plants such as seaweeds that normally live between high and low tides often grow higher up on the shore, sometimes as far as the trees in places like Big Sur.*

The first example is dry, the second flowery, and the third straightforward and accessible. Use technical terms only when their meaning cannot otherwise easily be "translated."

SENTENCE STRUCTURE

Most writing is composed of a series of sentences. Most good expository writing—writing that explains—uses a combination of sentences of different lengths. Variety is the spice of both life and good writing. Try mixing up short, long, medium, very long, and extremely short sentences. Sentences that are all very short will make your writing sound like Dick and Jane readers. A sequence of extraordinarily long sentences will confuse your reader. And a conglomeration of medium-length sentences will bore your reader. Use the active voice primarily. The passive voice is weak. In the active voice, the subject is acting. In the passive voice, something is being acted upon.

> *Passive: Getting ready for school is done by homeless children in public rest rooms.*
> *Active: Homeless children get ready for school in public rest rooms.*
> *Passive: The fast-draw was used by Wyatt Earp at the OK Corral to kill the Daltons.*
> *Active: Wyatt Earp used the fast-draw at the OK Corral to kill the Daltons.*

Notice that the examples using the active voice require fewer words. Sentence openings are either strong or weak, too, depending on whether the subject leads a sentence or is buried within:

> *Weak: In whale migration, the whales move south in the winter.*
> *Strong: Migrating whales move south in winter.*

Although writing that always begins with the subject can be effective in fiction (for example, in the work of

Ernest Hemingway or Richard Wright), it would be monotonous in the kind of writing you are doing. So begin some sentences with prepositional phrases and subordinate clauses:

> *To better understand the plight of the homeless student, we . . .*
> *Although the* Titanic *was considered unsinkable . . .*
> *In* Hamlet, *Shakespeare . . .*

Using the passive voice occasionally is not a bad thing and, in fact, will be inevitable: some ideas need to be expressed in this way.

PARAGRAPH STRUCTURE

Paragraphs are the major building blocks in writing term papers. Each expresses a group of related ideas, or fleshes out one small idea. Vary the length of your paragraphs in the same way that you vary the length of your sentences. One-sentence paragraphs are effective—when not overused. Use them to emphasize certain points.

As with sentences, there are both strong paragraphs and weak ones. In "strong" paragraphs, the main idea is stated at the beginning or at the end. In "weak" ones, the main idea is buried in the middle.

Although you probably have learned all about topic sentences, some writers do not use topic sentences in their paragraphs. In fact, in magazine articles many paragraphs are loosely constructed. Paragraphs often have one main idea, but in magazines such as the *New Yorker,* some paragraphs contain enough ideas to make your English teacher scream.

Unless you feel very confident in your writing, avoid huge paragraphs, and make your paragraph's main idea very apparent—which usually means putting it at or near the beginning of a paragraph.

THE FIRST PERSON

Is it okay to write in the first person? There are places in this book where I wanted to use the first person, but I avoided doing so because it seemed inappropriate.

The preceding paragraph could have been phrased to avoid using the first person: "There are places in this book where use of the first person was appealing, but seemed inappropriate."

There may be times when "I" is, indeed, called for, but think long and hard before actually going ahead and using it.

Now that you know a little more about some of the qualities of good writing, it is finally time to write!

SUPER STRATEGY

Computer programs such as Grammatik (Reference Software), Sensible Grammar (Sensible Software), and Correct Grammar (Wordstar) will review your writing style. They perform such functions as: checking on subject-verb agreement, commenting on passive voice use and paragraph length, and even telling you to which audience your writing is geared. They can be used in conjunction with popular word processing programs.

ELEVEN

ORGANIZING YOUR INFORMATION AND WRITING THE ROUGH DRAFT

At this stage, writing means writing a first—or rough—draft of your paper. Using your outline as a guide, you will be combining ideas and facts from your different sources and getting these ideas to flow in a smooth, organized fashion.

Keep in mind the points made in the short lecture on writing, but be more concerned with content and organization than with style. That is why this first version of your paper is called a rough draft. Don't worry too much now about breaking up your paper into formal sections. You will polish your writing and attend to organizational details later.

If you have followed the steps outlined in the previous chapters, you should be in pretty good shape at this point. You will have most of your cards in little (or big) piles or database fields organized by reference source. You also may have a small pile of notes to yourself: "Highlight the fact that Greenpeace does such and such," or "Not sure about cost of busing homeless children."

SORT AND ORGANIZE YOUR NOTE CARDS

The first thing to do with your note cards—or database fields—is to sort them by subject. If you have coded the cards by subject topics already, your task will be relatively easy.

Now organize the cards in each subject pile according to the order of topics in your outline. For instance, if you are writing about five black American artists, now is the time to pull out all the cards on the five artists and arrange them by exhibits, views, childhood, training, and so forth.

In sorting your cards, you may decide you want to rearrange the order. Don't do this yet. Just make a note on a card and put the card in front of the card or group of cards you may want to rearrange: "Move before last section?" When you have sorted all the cards according to your original plan, then you can change the order. But first rearrange the outline, which is your master plan. Your task will be a breeze if you wrote the outline using a word processor.

While sorting the cards the first time, you will undoubtedly see gaps in your information. You might write yourself a note on a card and slip it in with the others, "Add date of homeless legislation here," or "Tell why blue whales need more food per ton of body weight than other animals."

If you answered questions jotted down earlier and have a pile of miscellaneous cards, now is the time to insert these cards into their proper places in the rest of your cards. Toss out notes to yourself once you have resolved them, set aside oddball cards, discard duplicates, tag cards that still contain contradictory information or questions, and do anything else necessary to streamline and solidify your notes. Try to clear up problems at this point, but don't stall because of one or two missing dates.

WRITE THE PAPER

You are now ready to write the paper, following the order of your note cards (which is the same as that of your outline).

Begin a new paragraph each time you present a new main idea. Use section headings to separate large blocks of related material, although you may not wish to keep these headings in the final draft. Squeeze in as many facts and ideas as you can, even if you decide later to eliminate some of them. Although it is not that hard to add material later, it is probably easier to cut material.

If you have taken notes using a database program, use the computer to group your electronic note cards by topic. Arrange the topics in the order in which you plan to write about them. With a printout of your ordered "cards," you essentially have the skeleton of your term paper. You then need to expand and connect the paragraphs.

If your database program and word processing program are compatible, you can transfer the information in the database to the word processing program. This will save you a step, and your "skeleton" term paper will be ready to work on, without your having to retype or re-word-process it. An integrated-software package—one that combines a word processing program with a database program—can be used instead of separate programs.

Some word processors are easier to use than others. The more efficient ones allow you to work with two or more files at once. You could display your outline at the bottom of the screen while composing the paper at the top. You could also use the file at the bottom as an electronic notepad while you are working on your paper at the top. You also might be able to display your notes and paper in progress at the same time, facilitating the insertion of quotations.

You may feel better about working on hard copy (the printout). Print everything out, creating what might be a very rough copy, with extra-wide margins and double or triple spacing, and write in your notes and changes just as you would if it were a typed or handwritten draft.

INTEGRATE AND ACKNOWLEDGE OTHER PEOPLE'S MATERIAL

You have included quotations and paraphrases of authors on your note cards. When writing the first draft, you must be absolutely clear in your use of this material. Keep only those quotes that really add to your paper. Beware of using too many quotations: you will not get a medal for your efforts. Incorporate short quotations into the sentence or paragraph, with the footnote number at the end:

> Younger children fare worse. A test of 48 Massachusetts preschoolers found "54 percent of the homeless youngsters had at least one major developmental lag, compared to 16 percent of the children with permanent addresses."[1]

Indent longer quotations and type or word-process them in a block style; introduce them by citing part of the reference:

> Not all homeless children live in shelters. According to Landau in The Homeless:
>
>> Some have tried living out of abandoned cars or have fashioned homes from large cardboard boxes in out-of-the-way spots. Many mothers have moved their children to and from railroad and bus stations each day

hoping to find warmth and food. Their children do not attend school. They have no permanent address and are not part of any school district. They do not worry about homework; their main concern is that of surviving another day unharmed.[2]

Handle paraphrased material, and quotations that are incomplete sentences, as follows:

According to Robins,[3] special schools in shelters are separate and unequal, therefore unconstitutional. Child-advocacy groups argue that these schools "cut children off from the mainstream and institutionalize the homeless."[4]

Number footnotes and put them at the bottom of the page on which the quote or paraphrase occurs, or else create "endnotes"—a section that eventually will go at the end of the paper. Follow your teacher's instructions on whether to use footnotes or endnotes.

If you put the footnote on the same page as the quotation or paraphrase, single-space it (at least in the final draft), and insert a blank line between the end of the text and the footnote. Skip lines between footnotes if you have more than one. Endnotes can be single- or double-spaced; follow your teacher's instructions.

Figuring out how much room to leave at the bottom of the page for footnotes is tricky. A word processor can simplify this task. Either way, you will have to count lines of text and footnotes, and do some estimating. Chapter 12 shows the correct form for a footnote.

A sample page from a term paper on the education of homeless children parents, getting their child enrolled is a feat that goes beyond their resources.[1]

Because of these issues, according to the National Coalition for the Homeless, ''about 250,000 children, roughly 40 percent of all homeless kids, attend school on an irregular basis or don't go at all.''[2] Those homeless students in the schools face many problems. They fall asleep at their desks because they don't sleep at night. Homework doesn't get done because of noise and disorder. The teachers suspect that many of these children ask for seconds at lunch because they probably had no dinner the night before. As one teacher observed, ''These kids have problems you can't even imagine. Being in school is the best thing in their lives.''[3]

There are many alternatives in planning for the education of the homeless child, but what is the best way? This paper will discuss various possible approaches to educating homeless children, focusing on New York City. It will compare the methods, looking at how well each meets the needs of the children, and the costs and the practicality of each method, and will, finally, make recommendations as to the best approach.

---

[1] E. Anne Eddowes and John R. Hranitz, ''Educating Children of the Homeless'' *Education Digest* 55 (October 1989): 15.

[2] Connie Leslie and Pamela Abramson, ''Can a Shelter Be a School?'' *Newsweek* 114 (January 23, 1989): 51.

[3] Anna Kosof, *Homeless in America* (New York: Franklin Watts, 1987): 70.

Paraphrase Correctly

You already know a little about paraphrasing, but this technique confuses even the best of writers. You can paraphrase an author's general views on a subject. You might say:

> Jones seems to believe that our present educational system is failing to serve the homeless child.[5]

Or you can paraphrase a specific passage. Here is such a passage, followed by two paraphrases:

> Educators worry that, as the number of homeless children grows, education for those children—without sharp increases in funding for Chapter I and Head Start—can only get worse, not better.

Paraphrase 1:

> Without sharp increases in funding for Chapter I and Head Start, educators worry that as the number of homeless children grows, education for those children can only get worse, not better.

This is a paraphrase, yes, but a bad one because it is too close to the original. You may as well quote the original.

Paraphrase 2:

> According to Smith,[6] education for the growing number of homeless children will get worse without sharp increases in funding for Chapter I and Head Start.

Watch out that your paper doesn't turn into a mass of footnoted paraphrases; this is as bad as a paper overburdened with quotations.

Perhaps the only time you can ignore this advice is when you are analyzing the work of an author. In discussing Richard Wright's *Native Son,* you might want to use quite a few quotes from the book. Refer back to chapter 9 and the chart on what should be paraphrased, summarized, or quoted.

WRITE CREATIVE BEGINNINGS AND ENDINGS

One of the hardest parts of writing any paper is writing the beginning. Many authors write the opening last, or rewrite it many times.

Your opening can be something standard, such as, "In this paper..." or something a little snappier: "Homelessness is devastating to children, taking a toll on health and emotional well being. The most critical problem many homeless children face, however, is denial of an education."

The second, followed by a presentation of your ideas, is closer in style to the openings for magazine articles, called leads. The lead is meant to grab the reader's attention and at the same time set forth the main idea of the article.

While your teacher may not like an opening that is too catchy, he or she will probably appreciate an opening that is more original than "This paper will examine how being homeless affects a child's education and present ways the problem is being solved." This kind of opening is likely to get you a sigh or a groan. Why not surprise your teacher, then, with something a little different!

Read some different types of openings in books, magazine articles, newspaper stories, and journal articles to see what you like and don't like. Here are a few different approaches:

Soccer is played and watched by more people in the world than any other sport. It is also the fastest-growing participation sport in the United States. Let's take a closer look at why so many people like this game.

Here is a scene that might occur in any classroom in America.

Architecture is said to be the one art to which Americans have made original contributions. In the past seventy years American architecture has greatly influenced the design of European buildings. Yet the architect who most influenced American architecture has never received full credit for his contribution. This architect is Louis Sullivan.

The same approach applies to the conclusion of your term paper. Traditionally, the ending of a paper provides you with a chance to tie things up neatly and perhaps draw conclusions from your research. You can also describe what you learned that you didn't know before. A conclusion can be one paragraph or several. You should know, however, that all an ending really has to do is . . . end. But if you can think of a better way to conclude than to just summarize, why not try it!

Your teacher will be falling asleep over the fifteenth paper that ends, "In this paper, we saw that many homeless children are denied a quality education. In conclusion, it is only fair to state that. . . ." Your snappy ending could jolt her out of her chair with a smile of relief: "There are no *easy* solutions to providing equal educational opportunities to homeless children, but as their numbers continue to mushroom, the problem will be here for years to come." This certainly sounds like a conclusion, but it adds something extra—a challenge.

Other examples of conclusions:

Overwhelming evidence shows that drinking and driving don't mix. This paper will have heightened the reader's awareness of what can happen when they do.

There is little we can do once a nuclear attack occurs. The strategy the world must adopt is to avoid one at all costs.

In the last example, the first sentence summarizes the contents of the paper (evidence that little can be done once a nuclear attack occurs), while the second sentence offers the author's considered opinion. It is a strongly stated opinion, too, as shown by the word *must*. In your conclusion, you can also suggest solutions for the problem you have investigated, suggest laws, rules, or regulations that might improve the situation in the future, or mention related problems that need to be solved or explored.

Look in magazines and newspapers for some ideas on ending your paper, but don't be surprised if you find that half the articles and stories have a cute ending, a twist, or no ending whatsoever! You may have to revise your opening and conclusion several times to get them just right.

PREPARE THE BIBLIOGRAPHY

Prepare a rough draft of your bibliography at this stage, even though you may later add or delete some of the entries. There are different types of bibliographies, and your teacher may specify the kind he or she wants:

1. All sources consulted are included, whether or not you actually used anything from them, for example, a quotation, in the paper.

2. Only sources cited in footnotes are included.
3. All sources cited in footnotes are included, along with other, selected sources.
4. None of the above.

If your teacher doesn't tell you the type of bibliography to do, try number one, which covers all the bases.

In the next chapter, you will find the correct forms to use for the entries in your bibliography.

SUPER STRATEGIES

1. After developing a focus, writing a rough draft is the most difficult part of a term paper project. When you begin writing, choose a comfortable place. Give yourself plenty of space to spread out your notes. Pick a time when you work best and play some energizing background music.
2. A selection from a quotation book such as *Bartlett's Familiar Quotations* may spark a beginning for your paper.
3. Photos dealing with your topic may add inspiration. Place them around you while you write.

TWELVE
HOW TO CITE REFERENCES

Endnotes or footnotes must be constructed in a certain way. So must the bibliography. The reason is so that people reading your paper will know the source of your ideas and facts—when that source is someone other than you.

ENDNOTE OR FOOTNOTE FORMAT

Each type of reference is listed in a slightly different way. The following formats are acceptable to many people, although your teacher may suggest another way to do this. Be sure to follow exactly the spacing, punctuation, and order of each item in the citation.

In the examples that follow, book and periodical titles are underlined. If you are working on a computer, you may be able to use italics, which is the preferred style.

Books with One Author
[1]Author's first name Author's last name, <u>Title</u> (place of publication: publisher, publication date), pages used.

EXAMPLE:

[1]Joan Johnson, <u>Kids Without Homes</u> (New York: Franklin Watts, 1991), 68–69.

Books with Two Authors

[2]First Author's first name First author's last name and Second Author's first name Second Author's last name, <u>Title</u> (place of publication: publisher, publication date), pages used.

EXAMPLE:

[2]Lois Stavsky and J.E. Mozeson, <u>The Place I Call Home: The Faces and Voices of Homeless Teens</u> (New York: Shapolsky, 1990), 16–17.

No Author Given

[3]<u>Title</u> (place of publication: publisher, publication date), pages used.

EXAMPLE:

[3]<u>Homeless in America</u> (Wylie, Tex.: Information Plus, 1989), 22.

Institution, Association, etc. as Author

[4]Institution, <u>Title</u> (place of publication: publisher, publication date), pages used.

EXAMPLE:

[4]Phi Delta Kappa Educational Foundation, <u>Educating Homeless Children</u> (Bloomington: Phi Delta Kappa, 1990), 6.

Editor as Author

[5]Editor's first name Editor's last name, ed., <u>Title</u> (place of publication: publisher, publication date), pages used.

EXAMPLE:

[5]Lisa Orr, ed., The Homeless: Opposing Viewpoints (St. Paul, Minn.: Greenhaven Press,1990), 83–84.

Encyclopedia Article, Signed

[6]Name of encyclopedia, year of edition, vol. "Title of article," by Author's first name Author's last name.

EXAMPLE:

[6]World Book Encyclopedia, 1988, vol. 9. "Homelessness," by Kim Hopper.

Encyclopedia Article, Unsigned

[7]Name of encyclopedia, year of edition, vol. "Title of article."

EXAMPLE:

[7]Academic American Encyclopedia, 1992, vol. 10 "Homelessness."

Article in Magazine

[8]Author's first name Author's last name, "Title of article," Name of magazine volume number of magazine (date of magazine): page numbers.

EXAMPLE:

[8]Amy Stuart Wells, "Educating Homeless Children," Education Digest 55 (April 1990): p. 30.

Pamphlets, Government Documents

[9]Name of agency, Title of pamphlet, date of publication, pages.

EXAMPLE:

[9]U.S. House of Representatives. Select Committee on Children, Youth, and Families. The Crisis in Homelessness: Effects on Children and Families, 1987, 4.

CD-ROM
[10]Title of CD-ROM, date, "Title of article."

EXAMPLE:

[10]The New Grolier Electronic Encyclopedia, 1992, "Homeless shelter."

Audiovisual Material
[11]Title (format), (Place of distribution: Distributor, date).

EXAMPLE:

[11]Life Without a Home (video recording), (Woodland Hills, Calif.: Fox/Lorber Associates, 1990).

Interviews
[12]Interview with First name of person interviewed Last name of person interviewed, organization, place of interview, date of interview, where transcript can be found (if available).

EXAMPLE:

[12]Interview with Jean Freed, Chicago Homeless Shelter, Chicago, October 15, 1992.

More information on endnotes and footnotes can be found in the following books:

Chicago Manual of Style, 14th ed., Chicago: University of Chicago Press, 1982.
MLA Handbook for Writers of Research Papers, 3rd ed., New York: Modern Language Association of America, 1988.
Turabian, Kate L. A Manual for Writers of Term Papers, Theses, and Dissertations, 6th ed., Chicago, University of Chicago Press, 1980.

BIBLIOGRAPHY FORMAT

Bibliographies are styled slightly differently from end-notes or footnotes. The main difference is that authors' names are always listed with the last name, first; periods are used instead of commas between items in the listing; parentheses are not used for the publication data for books; and page numbers are not cited. In a bibliography, a source is listed once. Endnote or footnote sources are cited throughout the paper.

Here is how a source would be cited, first as a note, then as a bibliographic entry:

[7] Jonathan Kozol, Rachel and Her Children: Homeless Families in America (New York, Crown, 1988), 56–57.

Kozol, Jonathan. Rachel and Her Children: Homeless Families in America. New York: Crown, 1988.

The information provided in a bibliographic entry enables the reader to easily find and evaluate the source.

Here is a list of formats. More can be found in the books listed for note formats on page 116.

Books with One Author
Author's last name, Author's first name. Title. Place of publication: publisher, publication date.

EXAMPLE:

Johnson, Joan. Kids Without Homes. New York: Franklin Watts, 1991.

Books with Two Authors
First Author's last name, First Author's first name, and Second Author's first name Second Author's last name. Title. Place of publication: publisher, publication date.

If you find you are missing some information when you put together your notes and bibliography, you can probably fill in the holes from the library card catalog.

EXAMPLE:

Stavsky, Lois, and J. E. Mozeson. The Place I Call Home: The Faces and Voices of Homeless Teens. New York: Shapolsky, 1990.

No Author Given
Title. Place of publication: publisher, publication date.

EXAMPLE:

Homeless in America. Wylie, Tex.: Information Plus, 1989.

Institution, Association, etc., as Author
Institution. Title. Place of publication: publisher, publication date.

EXAMPLE:

Phi Delta Kappa Educational Foundation. Educating Homeless Children. Bloomington, Ind.: Phi Delta Kappa, 1990.

Editor as Author
Editor's last name, Editor's first name, ed. Title. Place of publication: publisher,copyright date.

EXAMPLE:

Orr, Lisa, ed. The Homeless: Opposing Viewpoints, St. Paul, Minn.: Greenhaven Press, 1990.

Encyclopedia Article, Signed
Name of encyclopedia, year ed., vol., "Title of article," by Author's first name Author's last name.

EXAMPLE:

World Book Encyclopedia, 1988, vol. 9., "Homeless-ness," by Kim Hopper.

Encyclopedia Article, Unsigned
Name of encyclopedia, year ed., vol., "Title of article."

EXAMPLE:

Academic American Encyclopedia, 1992, vol. 10, "Homelessness."

Article in Magazine
Author's last name, Author's first name. "Title of article." Name of magazine, date of magazine, pages numbers.

EXAMPLE:

Wells, Amy Stuart. "Educating Homeless Children," Education Digest, April 1990, 30–33.

Pamphlets, Government Documents
Name of agency. Title of pamphlet, date.

EXAMPLE:

U.S. House of Representatives. Select Committee on Children, Youth, and Families. The Crisis in Homelessness: Effects on Children and Families, 1987.

CD-ROM
Title of CD-ROM, date, "Title of article."

EXAMPLE:

The New Grolier Electronic Encyclopedia, 1992, "Homeless shelter."

Audiovisual Material
Title (format), Place of distribution: Distributor, date.

EXAMPLE:

Life Without a Home (video recording), Woodland Hills, Calif.: Fox/Lorber Associates, 1990.

Interview

Last name of person interviewed, First name of person interviewed. Organization, place of interview, date of interview.

EXAMPLE:

Freed, Jean. Chicago Homeless Shelter, Chicago, October 15, 1992.

SUPER STRATEGIES

1. If you have forgotten to record all the information you need for your reference, and you go back to the library and the book is checked out, do not panic! You should be able to get all the material you need for your bibliography from the catalog card, on-line catalog screen, or periodical index.
2. Reminder—a bibliography should be arranged in alphabetical order, by author.

THIRTEEN
REVISING THE ROUGH DRAFT; WRITING THE FINAL DRAFT

A rough draft is just that: a rough draft. The idea was to get your ideas down on paper in approximately the form you wanted them to take.

Writing from your note cards or computer "cards" sounded easy: Just construct a string of paragraphs, follow a few of the suggestions on writing, add a beginning and an ending, and bingo— a brilliant term paper. As you may have found out, writing a *good* rough draft involved a bit more effort.

MAKING REVISIONS

After completing the rough draft, read it. Read it critically, but also try to be nice to yourself. If you are too critical, you will feel discouraged. If you think the first draft is just wonderful and needs no additional work, you're probably deluding yourself. Almost all writers revise. Revising is not a sign of weakness or stupidity, just a fact of writing.

Some writers revise very little. They feel good about

the first draft, make a few changes, and, indeed, wind up with a good piece of writing. This goes for both students and professional writers. Other writers revise the first draft quite a bit, retype (or re-word-process), and are happy with the second draft. But a lot of writers, both students and professionals, revise even more. They may sometimes do two or three or four, or even more, drafts.

It is not the number of drafts that matters but the quality of writing and the quality of the revision. If you know how to revise and know good writing, you will be on the road to writing a good term paper.

The best way to learn to recognize the qualities of good writing is to read a lot, and to read both good and bad writing. Your English teacher should be able to give you suggestions. By studying both good and bad writing and comparing it with your own writing, you will get a sense of how good your first draft is and how much revising is necessary to turn it into a better piece of writing.

Most students don't revise enough. With this in mind, you should be able to streak ahead of your fellow students by revising a little more than you normally might be inclined to do.

READ FOR CONTENT

Read your paper once again, this time more carefully.

Have you included enough information so that your presentation is clear and complete? Have you written enough or too much? Are your ideas and facts all there? Are they well organized? Are there gaps or un-answered questions? Make notes in the margin: "How did the homeless senior get to the prom?" "Add details of welfare hotels." "Explain the effects of hunger more clearly." You may have to search your notes for the necessary information or even return to the library to do additonal research.

Go back now and make the necessary changes. If you used a computer, your task will be easier than if you typed or used pen or pencil for the first draft. Either way, you will need to add, delete, and shift the order of material. If you didn't use a computer, you will have left lots of space between lines when you typed or wrote the rough draft; for typists, this means triple-spacing and leaving wide margins. You may have to cut and paste to insert and rearrange whole paragraphs.

Strengthen Transitions

A collection of paragraphs containing a single idea per paragraph and following the order of your outline will probably wind up sounding like a series of discon-nected ideas. What's missing? Why, transitions, of course.

You need to connect your paragraphs so that ideas flow smoothly. To do this, you may have to add or subtract paragraphs and rearrange the existing para-graphs. You may also have to rethink your main ideas. You most certainly will have to add transitional sen-tences and words to link paragraphs.

Here are two paragraphs from a term paper written by a high school student. Note that the connection between the following two paragraphs is not very clear:

Homeless children face obstacles in trying to look, and be, like their classmates. It is nearly impossible for someone in extremely difficult circumstances to remain neat and clean. Homeless children may have no place to wash except for public rest rooms in parks and bus terminals. Some wear all the clothes they own on their body day after day. Many withdraw in class, because they can't relate to students with homes.

Hunger affects homeless children's school performance in that malnourished children are often weak, tired, irritable, cannot concentrate, and are susceptible to frequent infections.

The solution the author of the term paper chose was to add the transitional word *another*, to relate the second paragraph back to the first paragraph, along with a few other words that essentially echo information provided in the first paragraph.

*Hunger, **another problem of the homeless**, affects school performance because malnourished children are often weak, tired, irritable, cannot concentrate and are susceptible to frequent infections.*

Such overlapping (the words in boldface) can create transitions between paragraphs.

Another way to connect paragraphs is to establish a movement of time, as you do in a narrative, when you tell a story:

First, they did this. Later, they did that. The following year, she went here. Then she went there. She wound up feeling as if she had never settled down. That led her back to her family.

In the above example, pretend that each sentence leads a new paragraph.

Transition words that connect sentences are also useful in connecting paragraphs: finally, in the meantime, in addition, for example, a telling example is, however, yet, another, and instead.

WILL YOU DIVIDE INTO SECTIONS?

If you didn't divide your paper into formal sections in your rough draft, you may want do so now. Sectioning usually works well in a long paper; in a short paper, it may be unnecessary. Sectioning is a good way to organize large chunks of information that may be hard to connect. However, too many sections can also fragment your paper. Even sections need transitions!

Your outline will suggest where to divide your presentation. You might look it over again.

READ FOR STYLE AND LANGUAGE

Now read the paper with an eye for style and language. Do you have strong transitions between sentences, or are your sentences just jotted down with no thought to how they work together?

Do you have too many big words? Too many small words? What about paragraph and sentence length? Is there some variety, or are all your paragraphs two sentences long, and all your sentences six words long? Random lengths will ensure variety: long, very long, medium, very short, short, very short, medium, medium, short, long—this sort of pattern (actually, a non-pattern) can be your guide.

Make the necessary changes.

CHECK YOUR FACTS

Check your facts. This is something you may overlook. You may assume you got everything right the first time. There is a possibility, however, that even if you took notes accurately, you mangled something when converting your notes into a rough draft.

Ideally, you should go through your note cards and

compare the facts with those in the paper. Since you have been adding, deleting, and rearranging material, it is possible that you will have made some mistakes. Check names and dates, and fix discrepancies. (You may have said the location of a homeless shelter is on 57th Street in one paragraph, and on 59th Street in another.) Make sure quotations are accurate and that paraphrases do not resemble quotations so closely that you are guilty of plagiarism.

CHECK SPELLING AND GRAMMAR

When in doubt about the spelling of a word, use your dictionary. Failure to do so is probably the cause of half the misspellings people make. Spelling-checker programs are available with most popular word processing programs. These will highlight possible spelling errors but do not always correct them for you. A spelling checker cannot tell you, either, whether you meant to write "led" or "lead," or "can" or "car." You must read through your paper yourself.

Look for dangling modifiers ("Looking in the freezer, the ice cream was melting." Was the ice cream looking in the freezer?), run-on sentences ("Gold was discovered in Nevada County and Joe raised horses but Sue didn't know the time of day they lived in a large house and made a lot of money"), and sentence fragments ("They lived in a house. And made a lot of money. From making jewelry."). Have you used words correctly? Did you remember to change "Its over there" to "It's over there" and "She gave the dog it's bone" to "She gave the dog its bone"?

Some computer programs can tell you how many times you used certain words in your paper. You may have the habit of using *thus* in every third sentence. The program will point this out to you. The search-and-replace function common in many word processing programs will also allow you to change all your misspellings of Wyat Earp to Wyatt Earp with little more than a couple of keystrokes.

PREPARE THE "WRAPPER"

The "wrapper" (for want of a better word) is the title page, the table of contents, and the lists of illustrations and tables, if you plan to have them.

Check with your teacher about how he or she wants the title page prepared. Usually, all you need is the title, your name, and the section number of your class. Everything should be centered.

Depending on the length of the paper, a table of contents may or may not be needed. A good rule of thumb is to include one for papers longer than ten pages. The table of contents should list all the main parts of your paper, including the introduction, chapters or sections, and lists of illustrations, tables, and graphs, and so forth, and the bibliography.

USE ILLUSTRATIONS, GRAPHS, AND TABLES ONLY AS NECESSARY

Illustrations (photographs, drawings, diagrams) may be an essential part of a paper on the feeding habits of whales but may be unnecessary in a paper analyzing the fiction of Toni Morrison.

Avoid using illustrations unless you are required to by your teacher, or if you need them to illustrate some of your points. Maps may be necessary when you are discussing how quickly tropical rain forests are disappearing. Diagrams may be essential if you are explaining how a house is built. Photographs can be useful when you are comparing styles of art, fashion, architecture, or automobiles.

NEW YORK CITY'S HOMELESS CHILDREN:
Educational Alternatives

In Partial Fulfillment
of the Requirements
for Junior Writing

---

by
Mary Ruth Taylor
April 21, 1995

A sample title page

Graphs, charts, and tables can be useful for presenting statistics such as the increase in the number of homeless families during the Reagan administration. Statistics are an excellent way of supporting various arguments.

Never cut illustrations out of library materials. Make photocopies instead. If you make your own drawings, use a black pen; avoid colored markers or crayons. Keep the drawings simple. Label the appropriate parts of the drawings in ink or with typed labels.

Title each illustration, table, graph, or chart, and place it as close as possible to the corresponding text. You also could number all your pictures and place them at the end of the manuscript, with corresponding numbers in the body of the text. Tables, charts, and graphs may be more effective if used within the text, however. You will have to leave room for them when you are typing or word-processing, unless you are using software that allows you to create and then incorporate graphs and tables into the text.

A scanner hooked up to your computer will allow you to electronically copy and "paste" photographs and other illustrations. This ensures exact placement of your illustrations within the paper, enables you to reduce or enlarge any illustration, and to insert labels or explanations.

Prepare a list of illustrations or tables, charts, and graphs, but only if you are including a number of them. To each, add the title, number of illustration or table, and page number where it appears in the paper.

TYPE OR PRINT THE FINAL DRAFT

Now type or print out the final draft of your term paper.

Leave margins of at least one inch on all sides, and always double-space all text, except notes (unless you are instructed otherwise). Margins of 10 and 65 on a typewriter are standard; 15 and 56 leaves enough room to put the paper into a folder or to punch holes for a binder.

If you are using a word processor, you can be fancy and center section titles, justify the text (making all the words along the right-hand margin line up), use italics or bold type for emphasis, and so forth. Although the resulting paper will, undoubtedly, look better than a typed paper, your grade will still be based on the contents rather than appearance. Use graphics discreetly and only to make the paper easier to read.

Use white paper only; if you type, use "bond" paper but not erasable bond, which smears. Type or print on one side of the page only. Use a fresh ribbon in your typewriter or printer.

Number each page in the upper right-hand corner or in the top center. Number each page except the title page, and assign numbers to any lists of illustrations or tables you include.

Staple the pages of the paper or place them inside a report cover.

A FINAL WORD

Even though term papers are usually required assignments, writing them can bring you many benefits.

You not only learn about a topic you may know little or nothing about, but you will also gain important skills in communications, finding information, organizing information, managing your time, and conveying information in written language.

Think, too, of the term paper as a challenge. And, finally, if you adopt a positive attitude toward the assignment, you may even have some fun along the way!

SUPER STRATEGIES

1. It is usually better to interpret graphs or charts in your own words, rather than just put them in your paper.
2. If you having difficulty with transition sentences, refer back to your thesis statement for guidance. Make the transitions support your original thesis.

CHECKLIST FOR COMPLETION

Choose a topic
Brainstorm topic
Visit library to check on amount of information
available
Narrow or broaden topic
Write summary paragraph and thesis state-
ment
Check with teacher for topic suitability
Read a general encyclopedia article
Identify key terms
Check card catalog
Check for periodicals
Check reference books
Check government documents and pamphlets
Check for primary sources
Interview experts
Prepare working bibliography
Read and evaluate information
Prepare outline
Tighten focus
Revisit library for specific information
Sort/organize information
Write draft
Revise draft
Write the final draft
Prepare bibliography
Prepare table of contents (if more than ten
pages)
Prepare title page

$\mathscr{F}$OR FURTHER READING

Bankhead, Elizabeth. *Write It! A Guide for Research.* Englewood, Col.: Libraries Unlimited, 1988.

Banks, Michael. *Word Processing Secrets for Writers.* Cincinnati: Writer's Digest Books, 1989.

Barzun, Jacques, and Henry Graff. *The Modern Researcher.* 5th ed. New York: Harcourt Brace College Publications, 1992.

Bernstein, Theodore M. *The Careful Writer: A Modern Guide to English Usage.* New York: Atheneum, 1965.

Brady, John. *The Craft of Interviewing.* New York: Random House, 1977.

Carey, Helen H. , and Judith E. Greenberg. *How to Use Primary Sources.* New York: Franklin Watts, 1983.

Carey, Helen H., and Deborah R. Hanka. *How to Use Your Community as a Resource.* New York: Franklin Watts, 1983.

Chicago Manual of Style. 14th ed. Chicago: University of Chicago Press, 1993.

Dalton, Rick. *The Student's Guide to Good Writing: Building Writing Skills for Success in College.* New York: College Entrance Examination Board, 1990.

Ellis, Barbara L. *Barron's How to Write Themes and Term Papers*. 2nd ed. Woodbury, N.Y.: Barron's 1981.

Lamm, Kathryn. *10,000 Ideas for Term Papers, Projects, Reports and Speeches*. 3rd ed. New York: Arco/Prentice-Hall Press, 1991.

McCormick, Mona, ed. *The New York Times Guide to Reference Materials*. Revised ed. New York: New American Library, 1988.

MLA Handbook for Writers of Research Papers. New York: Modern Language Association of America, 1988.

Mulkerne, Donald J. D. *The Perfect Term Paper Step by Step*. New York: Anchor Press, 1988.

O'Brien, Geoffrey, ed. *The Reader's Catalog*. New York: Jason Epstein, 1989.

Provost, Gary. *100 Ways to Improve Your Writing*. New York: New American Library, 1985.

Semmelmeyer, Madeline, and Donald O. Bolander. *Instant English Handbook*. Chicago: Creative Publishing, 1986.

Strunk, William, Jr., and E. B. White. *The Elements of Style*. 3d ed. New York: Macmillan, 1979.

Turabian, Kate L. *A Manual for Writers of Term Papers, Theses, and Dissertations*. 6th ed. Chicago: University of Chicago Press, 1980.

Vernolia, Jan. *Rewrite Right!* Berkeley, Cal.: Ten Speed Press, 1987.

Vernolia, Jan. *Write Right!* Berkeley, Cal.: Ten Speed Press, 1988.

Wynar, Bohdan S., ed. *Recommended Reference Books for Small and Medium-Sized Libraries and Media Centers*. Englewood, Colo.: Libraries Unlimited, 1991.

ℐNDEX

Page numbers in *italics* indicate illustrations

Abbreviations, use of, 90
Active voice, 99
Almanac(s), *37*, 50
Alphabetizing, methods of, 41
America Online, 47, 67
American Topic Finder, 27
Animals and plants, standard reference books on, 51
Association as author, 114, 119
Atlas(es), *37*
Audience, writing for, 95–97
Audiovisual material, 116, 120–21
Author(s), 113–14, 117–19

Bartlett's Familiar Quotations, 112
Beginnings, writing, 109–10
Bibliographic Retrieval System (BRS), 21, 47, 48, 63
Bibliographies, 74–78, 111–12, 117–21
Biographies, 38, 56–57
Books, 113–14, 117
Brainstorming, 25–26
Brainstorms and Blueprints (Stripling/Pitts), 91, 94

Card catalog, 21, *22*, 40–46, *118*
CD-ROM (Compact Disc/Read-only Memory), 21, 47, 48, 63, 116, 120
Chart, as outline, *85*
Checklist, 133

Chemistry, standard reference books for, 57–58

Chicago Manual of Style, 116

Clustering, 23–25

Cluster map, 83, *84*

Community resource file, 69

Compton's Multimedia Encyclopedia, 48

CompuServe, 47, 48

Computer(s), 9–10, 27–29, 40, 77–78, 101, 104, 127–28

Computer formats, 47–48

Computer programs, 78, 89, 101

Content, 123–25, 128

Correct Grammar, 101

Courtesy, 71–73

Cross-references, 43

Databanks, 47, 63–65

Database(s), 47–48, 88–89, 104

Dewey Decimal system, 38

DIALOG, 47, 48, 63

Documents, 40, 115, 120

Earth and space, standard reference books for, 52

Economics, standard reference for, 52–53

Editor as author, 114, 119

Encyclopedias, 27, *37*, 47–48, 115, 119–20

Endings, writing, 110–11

Endnotes, 106, 113–17

Events/history, standard reference books for, 53

Facts, 91, 126–27

Fiction, organization of, 38

Final draft, writing, 130–31

First person, use of, 101

Footnotes, 105, 106, 113–17

"Full-text" databases, 66

Grammar, checking, 127

Grammatik, 101

Graphs, 128, 130

Hard copy, 105

History, standard reference books for, 53

Humanities, standard reference books for, 53–55

Humanities Index, 61

Ideas and issues, reference books for, 55–56

Illustrations, 93–94, 128, 130

Index cards, uses of, 77, 83, 88, 118

Indexes, 63–66
  See also Periodical indexes
Information, 91–92, 102–3
Information Finder, 48
InfoTrac, 63
Institutions as author, 114, 119
Interlibrary loan, 61, 66
Interviews in bibliography, 116, 121
Inventions, references for, 56
Italics, use of, 113

Jargon, 97–98

Key terms, 33–34, *35*

Lamm, Kathryn, 27
Language, 98, 126
Leads, 109
Letter-by-letter alphabetizing, 41
Library, 36–67, *17, 32, 37, 54,* 78, *81*
Library of Congress, 38
Library of Congress Subject Headings, 34

Machines, standard reference books for, 56
Magazines, *28,* 38, 115, 120
  See also Periodicals

Magazine Article Summaries, 63
Manual for Writers of Term Papers, Theses, and Dissertations (Turabian), 78, 116
Medicine, standard reference books for, 57–58
Microfiche, 21
  readers, 38–40, *39*
Microfilm readers, 38
MLA Handbook for Writers of Research Papers, 116
Modem, defined, 47
Modern Language Association, 78, 116

Names, in card catalog, 44
Narrowing, techniques for, 23
New Grolier Multimedia Encyclopedia, The, 48
New York Times Index, The, 27, 38
New Yorker, 100
Nonfiction, 38
Notes and note taking, 31–33, 86-*94,* 103, 104

On-line catalogs, 21, 44–46
On-line encyclopedias, 47–48
On-line indexes, 63–66

On-line catalog, *42, 45*
Openings, 109–10
Opinions, evaluating, 91
Opposing Viewpoints, 75
Oral histories, 69
Other people's material,
  105–9
  See also Paraphras-
    ing; Quotations
Outline(s), 30–33, *32,*
  79–85

Pages, numbering of, 131
Pamphlets, 50–51, 115,
  120
Paragraphs, 126
Paragraph structure,
  100–101
Paraphrasing, 92–93,
  106, 108–9
People
  as primary source,
    71
  standard reference
    books for, 56–57
Periodicals, 58–62, *59,*
  64
  See also Magazines
Periodical indexes, 21,
  34, 58–62
Permissions, 71–73
Photocopies, 58, 88
Physics, standard refer-
  ence books for, 57–
  58
Places, standard refer-
  ence books for, 57

Plagiarism, 46, 92
Planning outline, *32*
Plants, standard refer-
  ence books for, 51
Primary sources, 68–73,
  70, 72
Pro-Cite, 77–78
Prodigy, 47, 48

Quotations, 92–93,
  105–6

*Random House Encyclo-
  pedia, The,* 48
*Readers' Guide to Peri-
  odical Literature,* 20,
  38, 60–61
  CD-ROM version of,
    63
Reference(s), 36–67, *37,*
  54, 113–21
Reference Shelf, The, 75
Research, 13–14
Research Paper Writer,
  78
Research Planner, 27–
  29
Revising, 122
Rough draft, 104–12,
  122–30
Rough notes, 31–33

Scanner, use of, 130
Scientific American, annual index of, 27
Search-and-replace
  function, 127–28

Sears List of Headings, 34
Secondary sources, 68, 76
Sections, 126
"See also references," 43
"See references," 43
Sensible Grammar, 101
Sentence(s), 126
Sentence structure, 99–100
Sifting, 88
SIRS. *See* Social Issues Resources Series
Social Issues Resources Series (SIRS), 62–63
Space, standard reference books for, 52
Spelling, checking, 127
Statistical Abstract of the United States, 50
Statistics, use of, 128
Style, 97, 126
Subject references, *37,* 48–50
Super Strategies, 11, 14, 29, 34, 66–67, 73, 78, 85, 94, 101, 112, 121

Table of contents, 128
Tables, 128, 130
"Teacher pager," 67
Technology, standard reference books for, 56

10,000 Ideas for Term Papers, Projects and Reports (Lamm), 27
Term paper, *8,* 12–14, *107*
checklist for, 133
topics for, 15–29
Term Paper Writer, 78, 89
"Thesaurus of Subject Headings," 34
Thesis statement, 30
Title(s), 44
Title page, 128, *129*
Tone, of writing, 97–98
Topic(s), 15–29
choices of, 20–25
final questions to ask, 29
personal interest in, 15–18
refining, 18–25
sources for, 27–28
for term papers, 15–29
Topic code, 90
Topic sentences, 100
Transitions, 124–25
Turabian, Kate, 78, 116

Values, evaluating, 91
"Vertical file," 50
Videodiscs, 73

Webbing, 23–25
Web map, 83, *84*

Word-by-word alphabetizing, 41
Word processors, 104
  See also Computer(s)

Wrapping, preparing, 128
Writing
  characteristics of
    good, 96–101
  little lecture on, 95–101